4000 Flower & Plant Motifs

4000 FLOWER & PLANT MOTIFS

A SOURCEBOOK

GRAHAM LESLIE McCALLUM

BATSFORD

First published in the United Kingdom in 2004 by
Batsford
10 Southcombe Street
London W14 ORA

An imprint of Anova Books Company Ltd

ISBN-13: 9780713489095
ISBN-10: 0 7134 8909 X

A CIP catalogue record for this book is available from the British Library.

10 9 8 7 6 5

Reproduction by Classicscan, Singapore
Printed and bound by SNP Leefung Ltd, China

Design by Lee-May Lim

This book can be ordered direct from the publisher at the website:
www.anovabooks.com, or try your local bookshop.

Distributed in the United States and Canada by Sterling Publishing Co.,
387 Park Avenue South, New York, NY 10016, USA

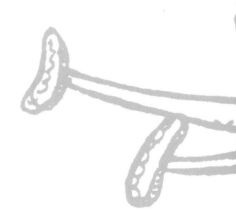

CONTENTS

Introduction   9

Mesopotamian   13

Egyptian   23

Greek   31

Romanesque   39

Byzantine   51

Medieval   57

Islamic   75

Chinese   89

Japanese   103

Folk   119

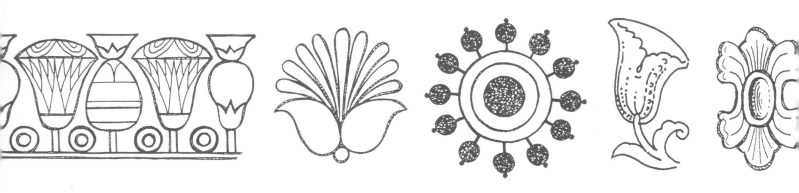

Art Nouveau 141

Art Deco 165

Flowers 177

Leaves 233

Fruit 257

Vegetables 289

Fruiting Bodies 311

Trees 333

Motifs 351

Borders 371

Index 376

INTRODUCTION

Are you an artist or a designer, or perhaps a lover of art? Are you maybe a craftsman, or possibly a keen hobbyist? Then this book has been created especially for you. Creative people are always searching for that perfect design, that ideal motif, that necessary inspiration that will give their artworks and their projects greater appeal. This book will prove to be a generous companion and a valued addition to your bookshelf.

Within these covers are over four thousand designs of plants, flowers, fruit and vegetables.You may copy or adapt any of them for your own purposes. One thousand nine hundred of these designs have been sourced from the generous artistic legacy of many hundreds of artists and designers, covering many historic and cultural styles and art movements. I have taken great care in drawing these designs, and in representing them to you in all their wonderful creative genius. This will aid you in reproducing the images, as well as in teaching you the different elements, principles and approaches to designing.

These images have been sourced from many locations, from the most exalted and visible, to the most simple and obscure. The beautiful buildings of the past, with their carvings, paintings and mosaics are veritable treasure chests of inspiration to the researcher. The stonemasons and sculptors of Egypt, Greece and Byzantium adorned the buildings they worked on with exquisite plant patterns and motifs. The Romanesque and Medieval stone workers laboured to the glory of God, erecting cathedrals of astounding beauty; bejeweled and laced in intricate carvings and images.

Another excellent source of designs are the naïve motifs of the home potters, weavers, and embroiderers of the past. Good examples of this are the everyday pottery utensils and vessels of the Chinese and Japanese; the intriguing weavings and knotted carpets of the desert tribes of the Middle East; and the charming embroideries of colonial North America. These images are very appealing to artists because of their simplicity and unaffected quality; the designs of the Chinese and Japanese for their minimalism, the Middle Eastern tribes for their geometrical abstractions, and the colonists of North America for their art's rustic homeliness.

The creative legacy of all the jewellers, carvers, painters, illuminators and smiths, from all the many different cultures of the past, including the Art Nouveau and the Art Deco movements, have generously contributed to this book. This charitable inheritance requires our humble gratitude.

The remaining two thousand eight hundred designs have been birthed in my own imagination and the creative endeavours of the last 33 years. I have retrieved designs from my childhood sketchbooks, from school and study projects, and from years of commercial activity. Most of the designs, however, come from the many hours that I spent happily and contentedly sketching and designing with no motive other than sheer pleasure.

Friends and colleagues, who used this collection of designs for their own creative pursuits suggested to me that they would make a successful and useful book.

This conclusion led me to spend two years studying the cultural styles of the past and to reproducing the designs that typify these styles. If this inception of the book was the seed, it was my deep and abiding love of plants that watered the project, thus growing the seed into a sapling, and finally nourishing it into a broadly branching tree.

Plants and flowers offer artists wonderful and free inspiration. We are surrounded by the floral kingdoms' many and marvelously varied treasures. All it takes is for you to open a window to your garden, or, for you to observe the pot plants on your desk, to be given creative inspiration.

Plant and flower design is a fascinating subject, for it too, opens a window to what other artists and designers have found to be inspiring. Almost every culture and art movement made use of plants as a creative source to embellish their artworks, clothes, jewellery and buildings. Some of these designs were passed from one artist to another, from the oldest civilizations, right down to our present time.

An interesting example of the transmission of a plant motif is to be found in the Middle East. The Mesopotamian cultures, such as the Sumerians and Babylonians, were among the first to use plant design. Their artworks, utensils and buildings were embellished with date palms, pomegranates and wheat. This signifies not only the plants' design worthiness, but also their importance as crops. Over time they transformed their date palm design, simplifying and abstracting it into what designers call a 'Palmette'.

The Egyptians used the palm as a design source too. The capitals that crown the tops of many a building's column were fashioned in the shape of a fountained palm. As a result of ancient commercial activity, the Greeks adopted the Palmette design, using it to decorate their pottery and buildings. Now, it sported a new name, the 'Anthemion'. The motif was then transferred from the Greeks to the Byzantines, and then on to Romanesque art. It later featured prominently in Islamic art, and the Renaissance. Eventually, it found its way to our generation, where it is a well-known image.

It is this transmission of ideas and inspiration from one individual to another and from one culture to another, over hundreds of years that is so exciting to historians and to botanists. To artists and designers, it has even greater interest. The techniques that were used in plant design, are not only lessons to creating our own designs, but also lessons in appreciating beauty, elegance and simplicity.

You will find this book to be very user-friendly. Different design styles have been richly illustrated, drawn in great clarity and detail, and have been neatly placed within chapters of their own. This will help you to discover what it is that gives a design style its individual character, look and feel. All designs are in black and white, as this facilitates their copying by hand or by electronic means, although please note that all the designs are for personal use only.

A comprehensive index allows you to locate any design subject, motif or pattern with speed and ease.

Design entices us to be acquisitive assimilators of inspiration, yet, it also places an obligation on us to be generous sowers of art. I hope that this book will inspire you to new and greater creativity.

MESOPOTAMIAN

A   B   C   D

E   F   G   H

I   J   K

A

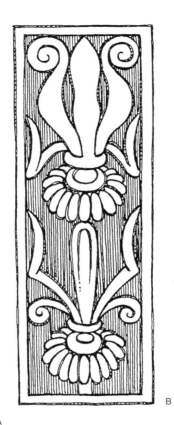

B

C

D

E

F

G

H

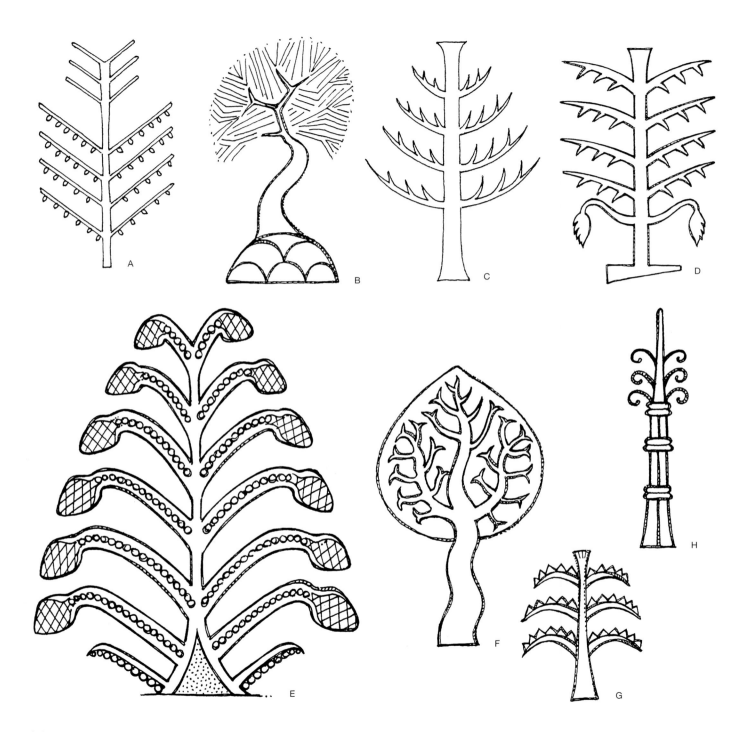

A   B   C   D   E   F   G   H   I

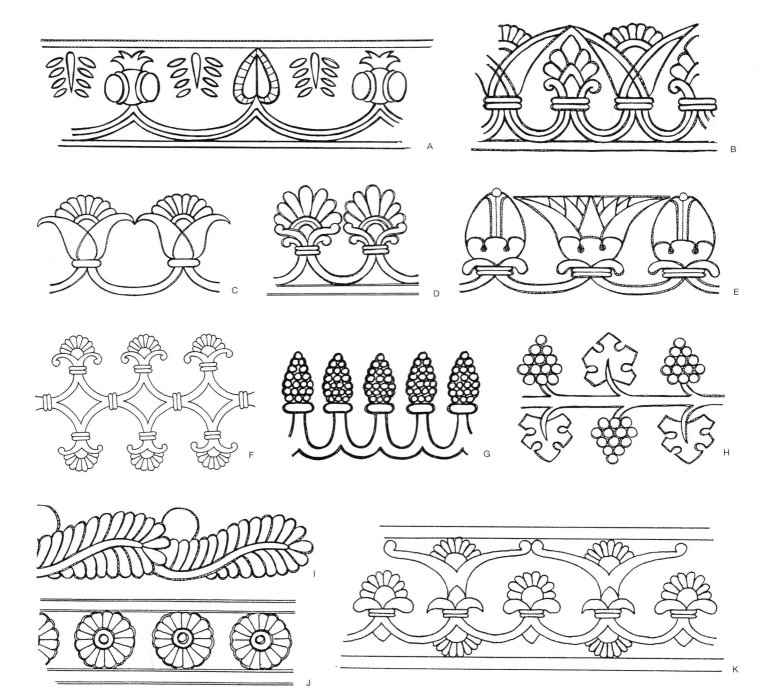

EGYPTIAN

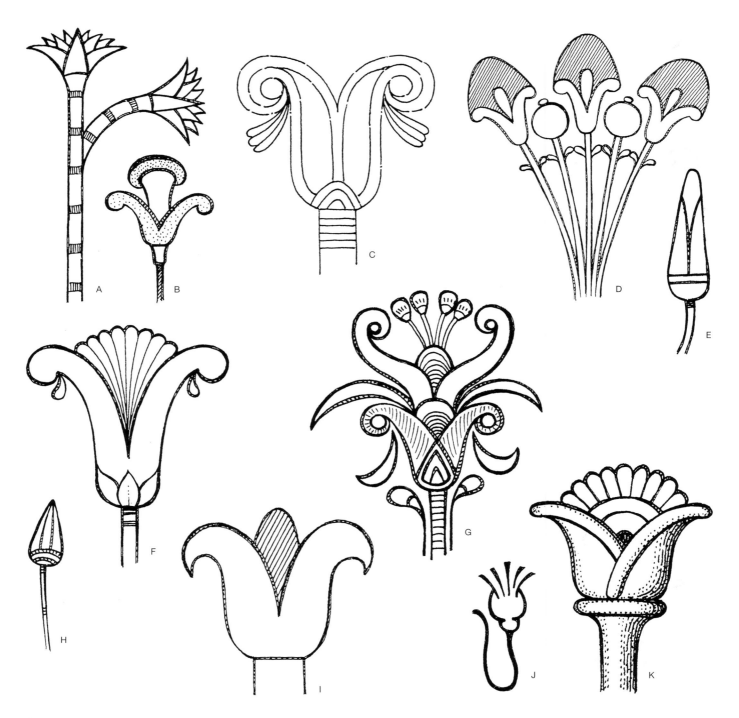

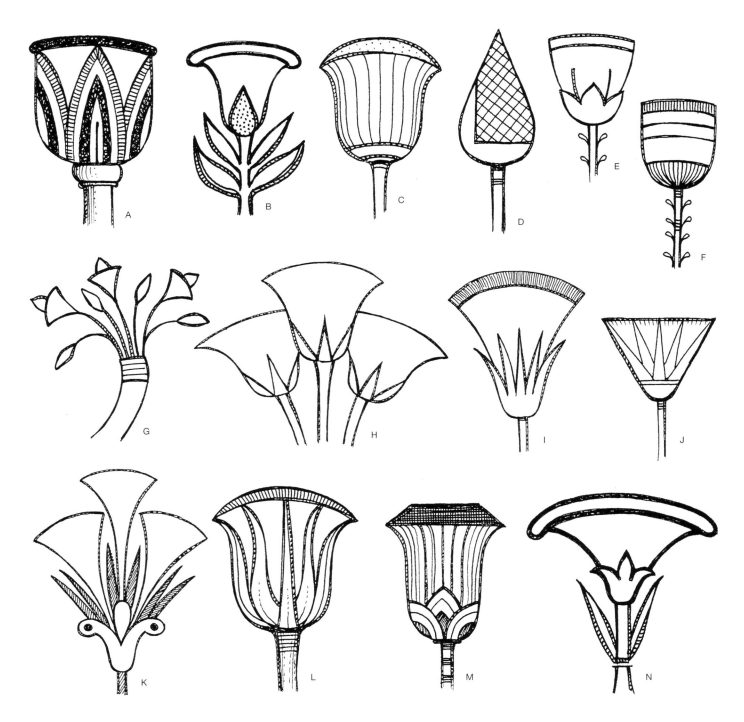

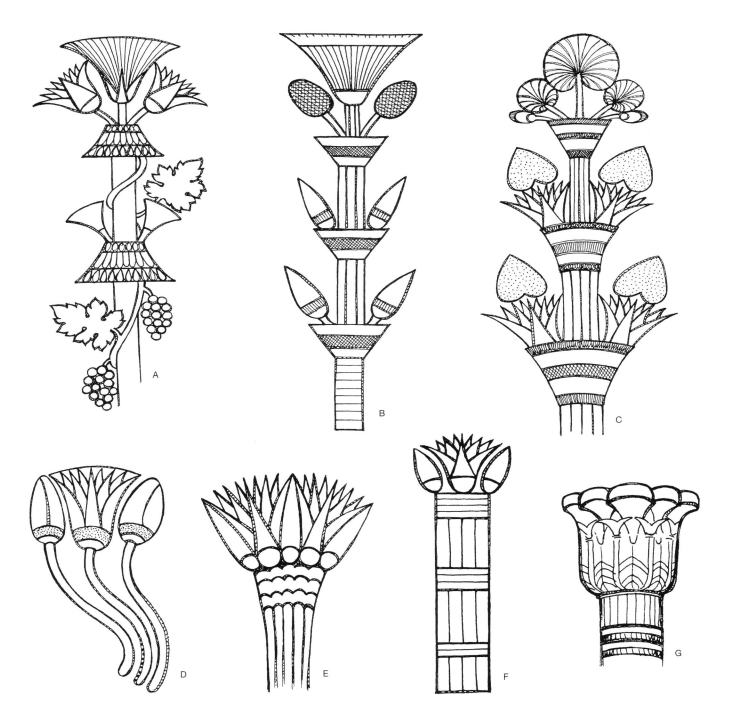

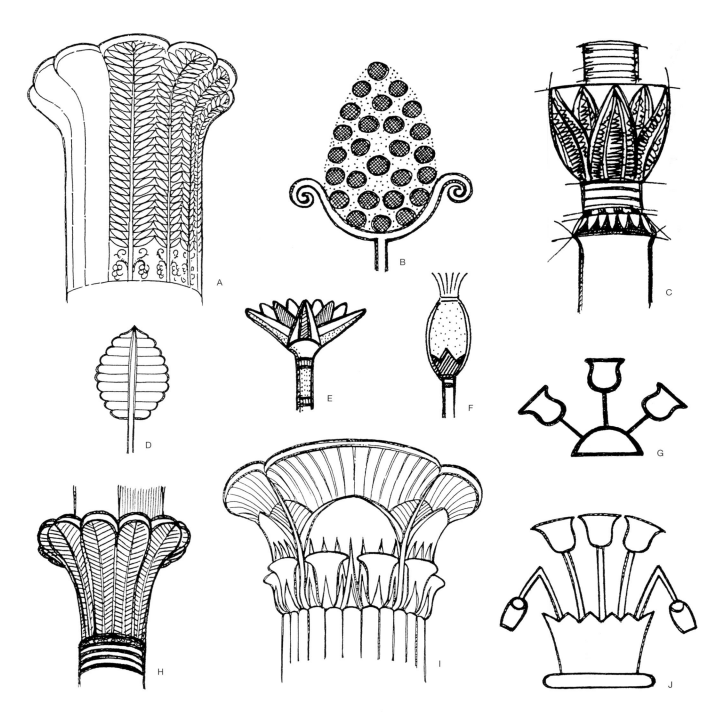

A

B

C

D

E

F

G

H

I

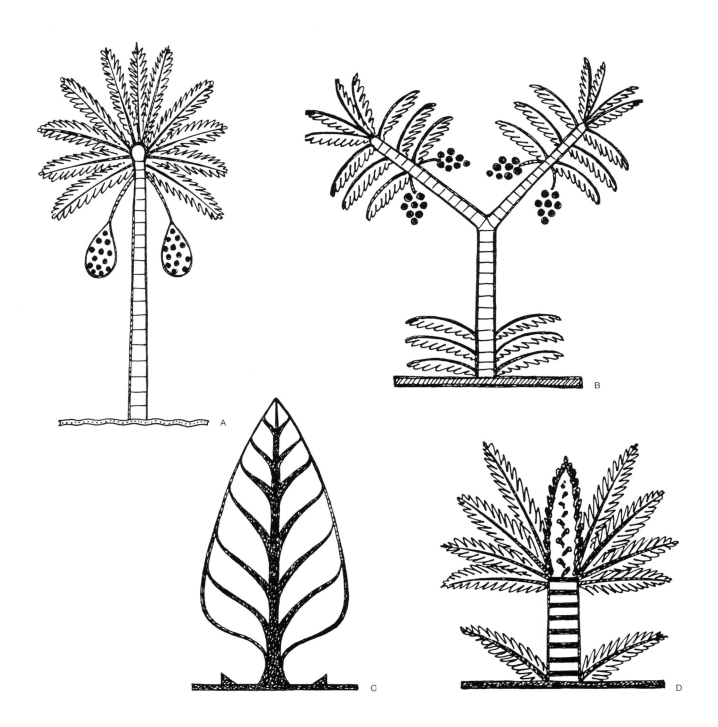

GREEK

A

B

C

D

E

F

G

H

I

J

K

L

M

A

B

C

D

E

G

F

H

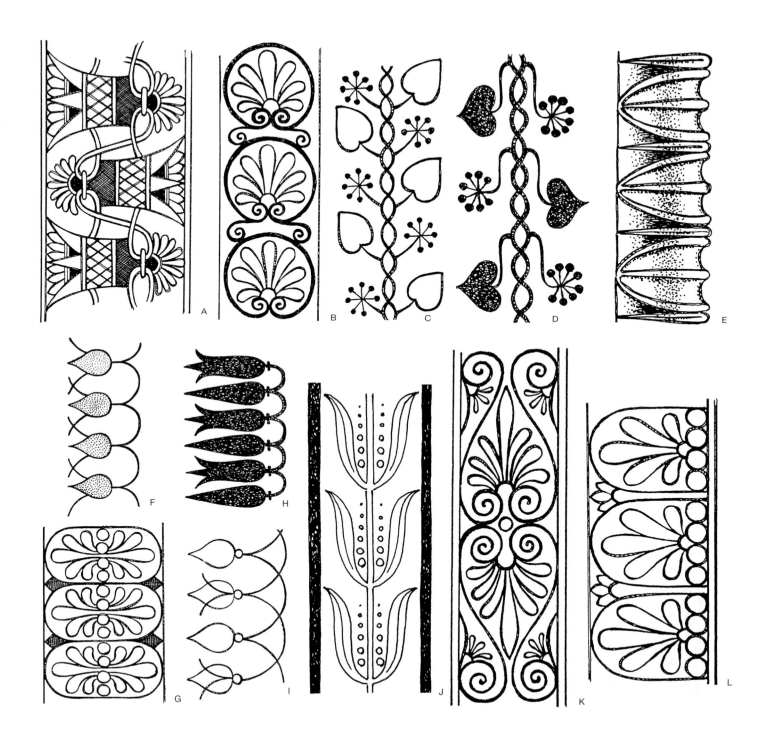

A B C D E

F H

G I J K L

A

B

C

D

E

F

G

H

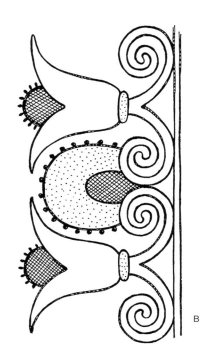

ROMANESQUE

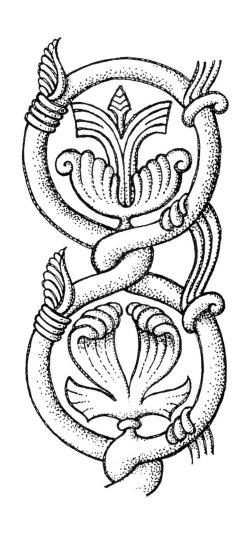

A

B

C

D

E

F

G

H

I

J

K

L

M

A

B

C

D

E

F

G

H

I

J

A

B

C

D

E

F

G

H

I

J

K

L

M

N

A B C D E F G H I J K

BYZANTINE

A

B

C

D

E

F

G

H

I

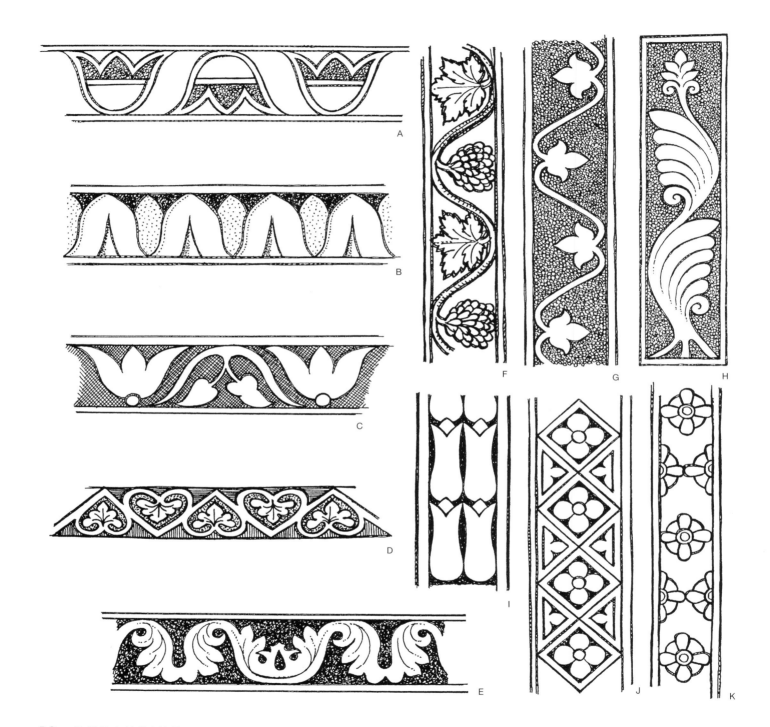

MEDIEVAL

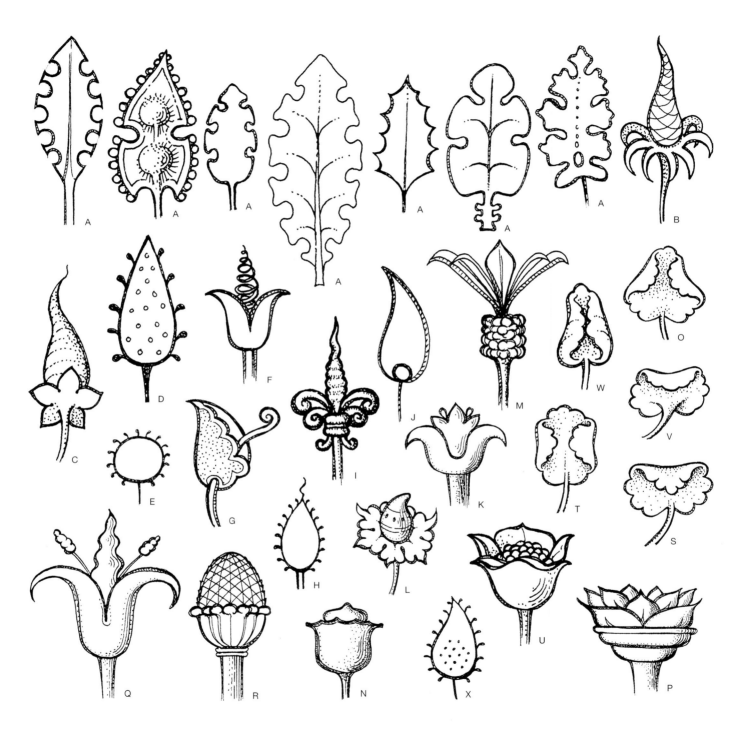

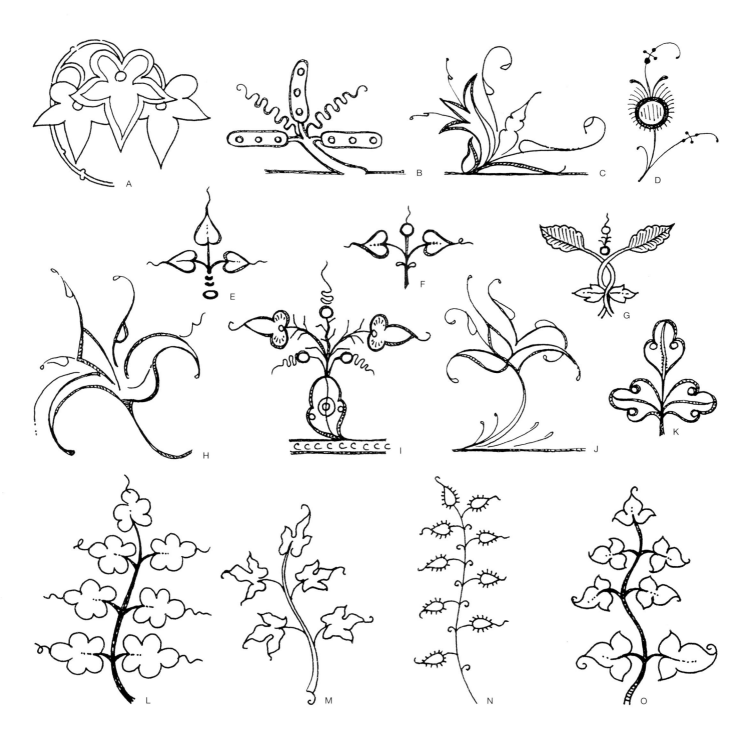

A

B

C

D

E

F

G

H

I

J

K

L

M

N

O

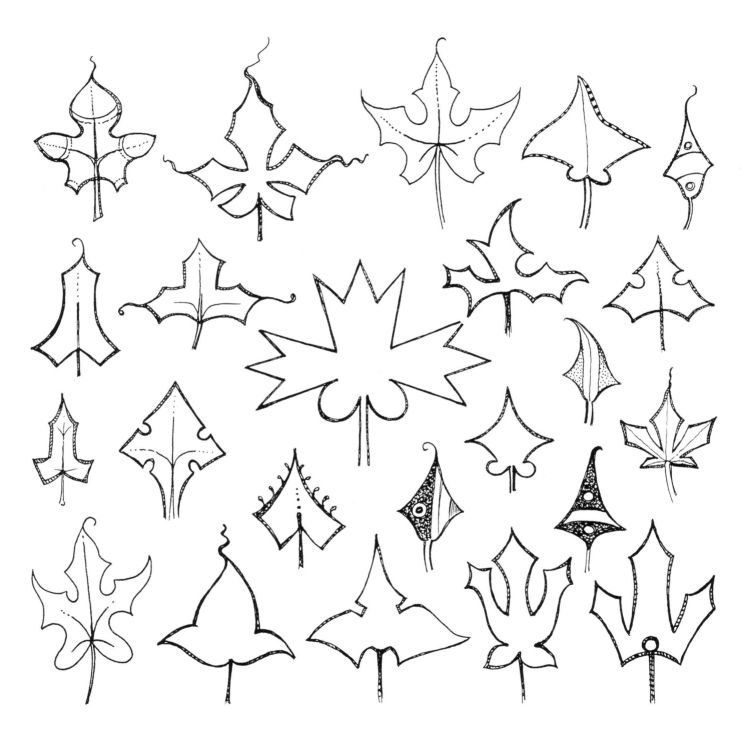

A B C D E F G H I J K L M N O P Q R S T U V W

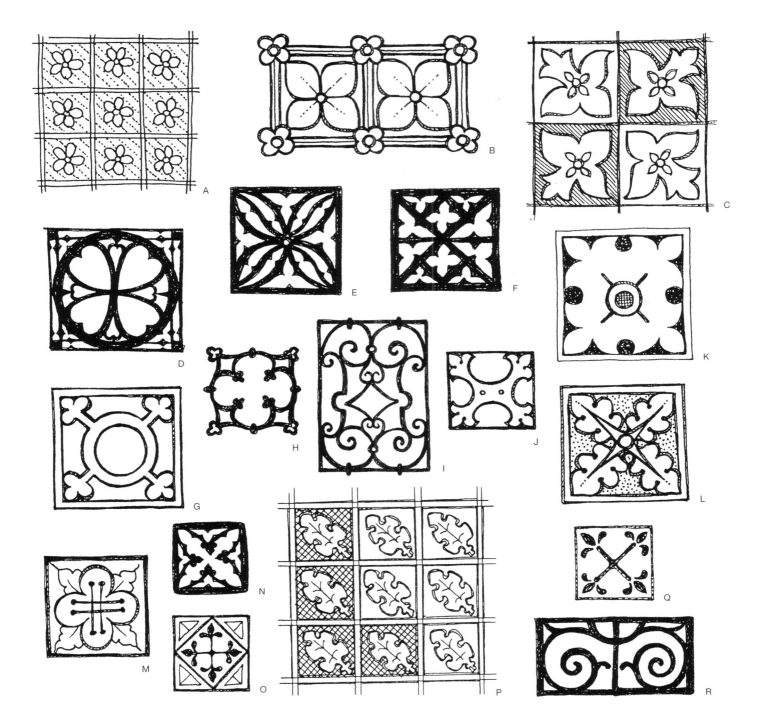

A

B

C

D

E

F

G

H

I

A

B

C

D

E

F

G

H

I

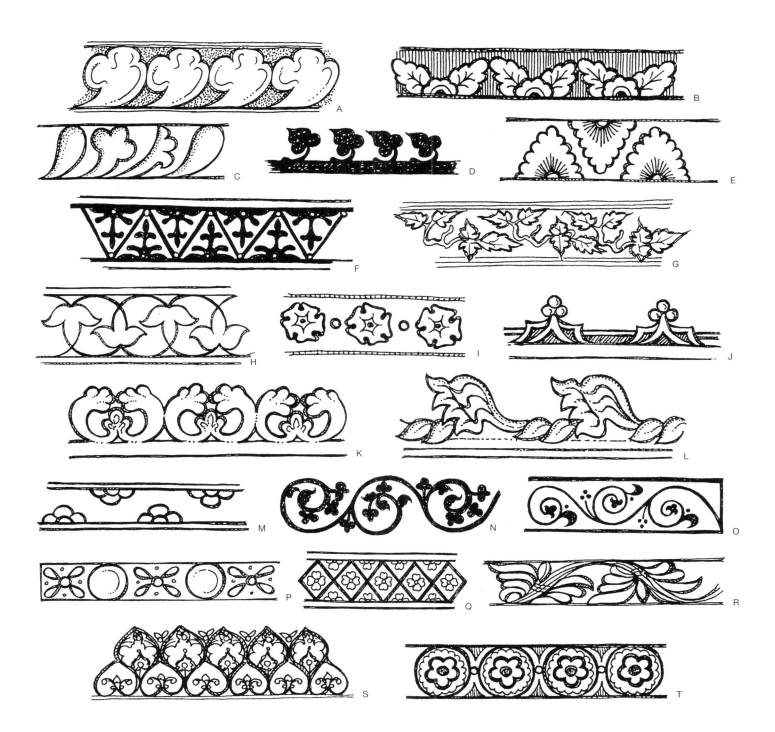

ISLAMIC

A B C D E F G H I J K L M N

A   B   C   D   E   F   G   H   I   J   K   L   M

A

B

C

D

E

F

G

H

I

J

K

L

M

N

O

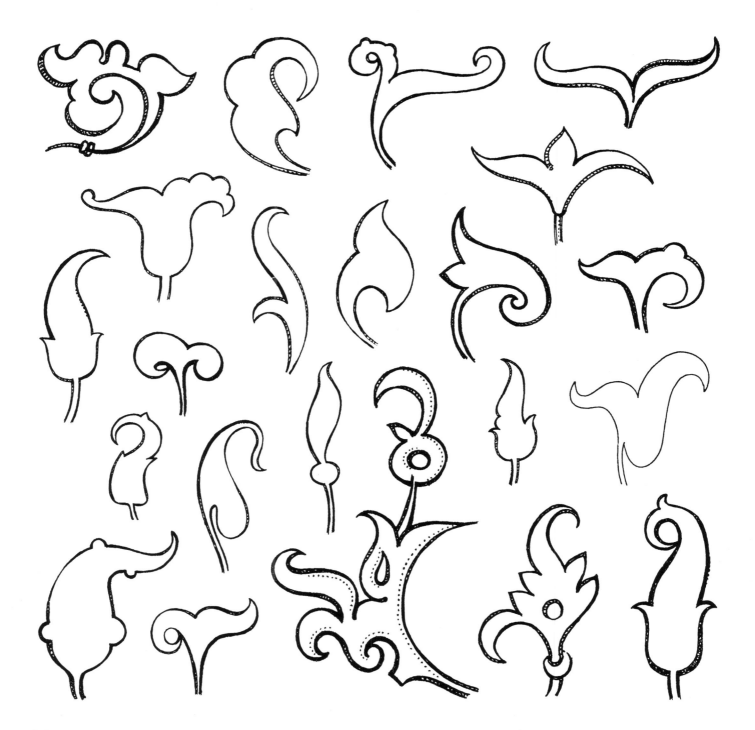

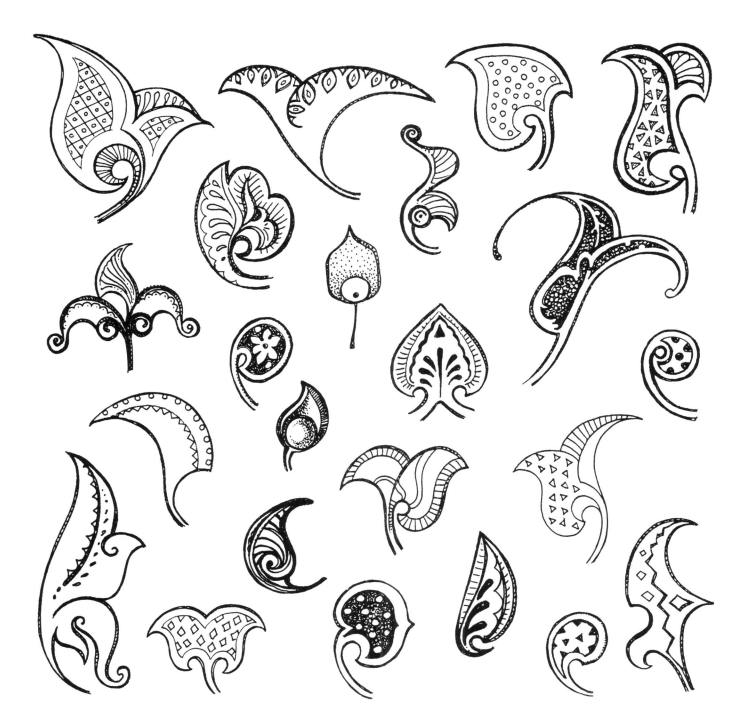

A

B

C

D

E

F

G

H

I

A

B

C

D

CHINESE

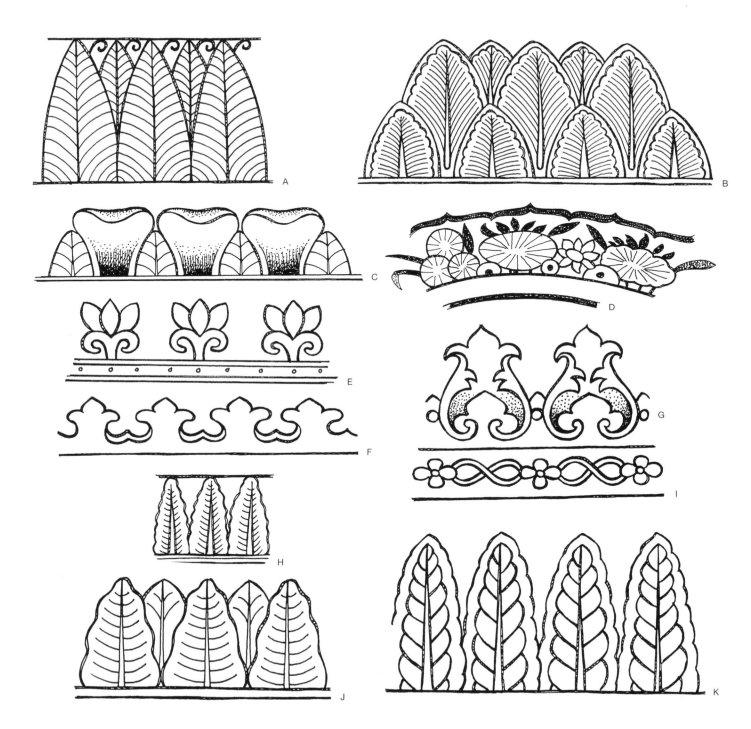

A

B

C

D

E

F

G

H

CHINESE 101

A

B

C D E F G

H

JAPANESE

A

B

C

D

E

F

G

H

I

J

K

L

A

B

C

D

E

F

G

H

I

A B C

D E F

G H I

A

B

C

D

E

F

G

H

I

J

K

L

M

FOLK

A   B   C   D   E   F   G   H   I   J   K   L   M   N

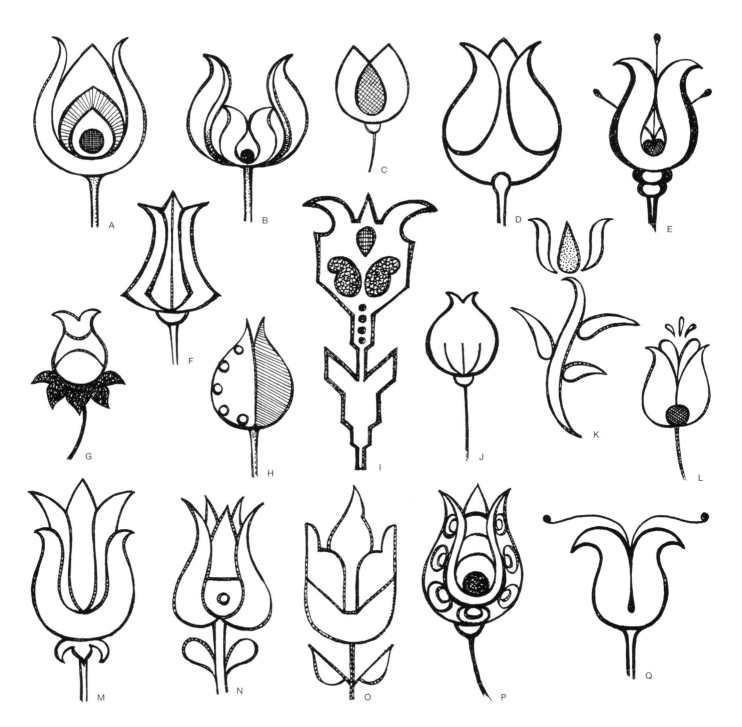

A B C D E F G H I J K L M N O P

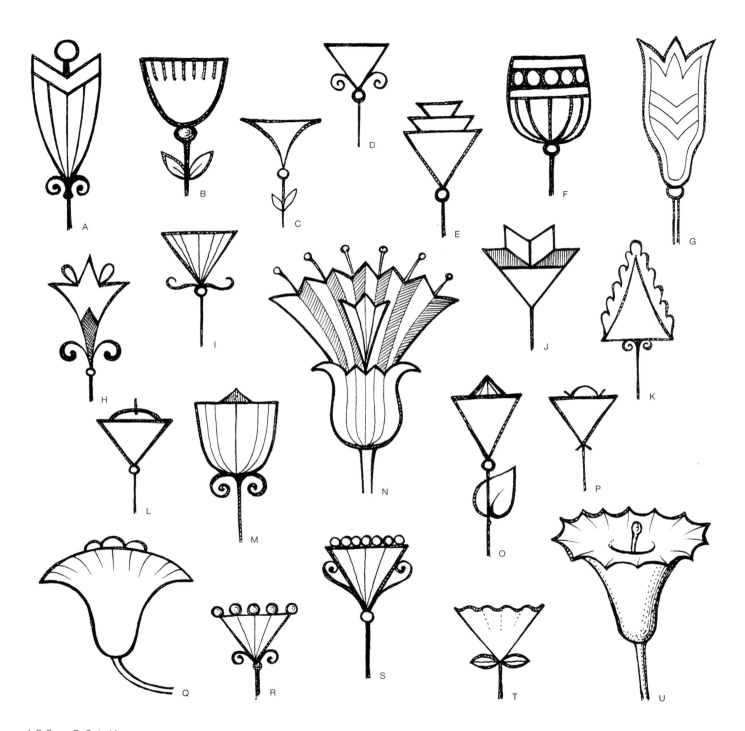

A

B

C

D

E

F

G

H

I

J

K

L

M

N

O

P

Q

R

S

T

U

V

W

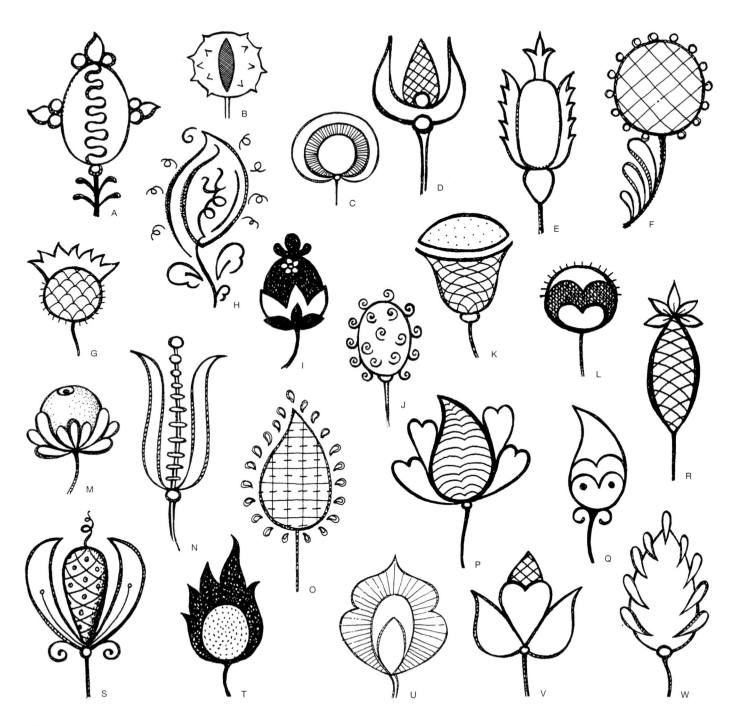

ART NOUVEAU

A

B

C

D

E

F

G

H

I

J

K

A

B

C

D

E

F

G

A

B

C

D

A

B

C

D

E

F

G

H

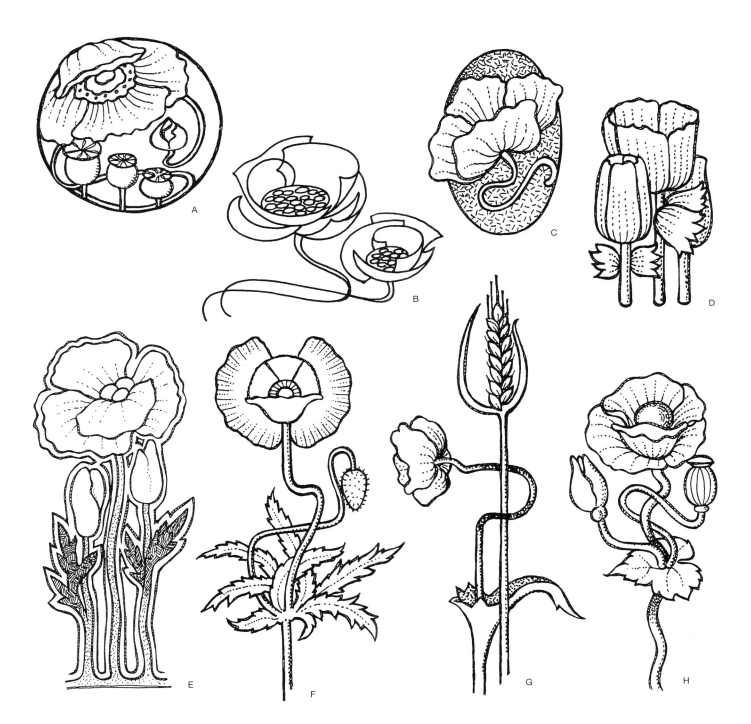

A B C D E F G H

A

A

B

C

D

E

F

G

H

I

J

A

B

C

D

E

F

A

B

C

D

E

F

G

152 ART NOUVEAU

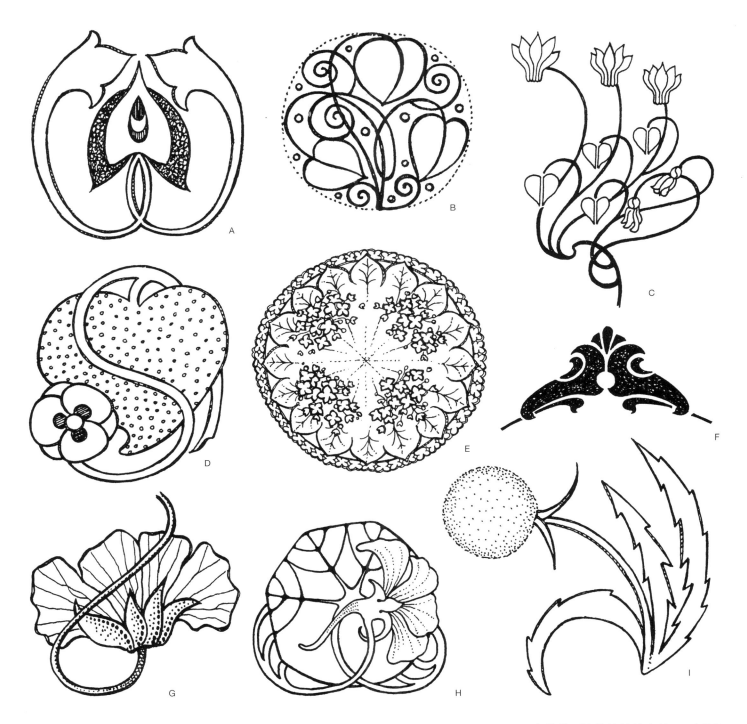

A

B

C

D

E

F

G

H

I

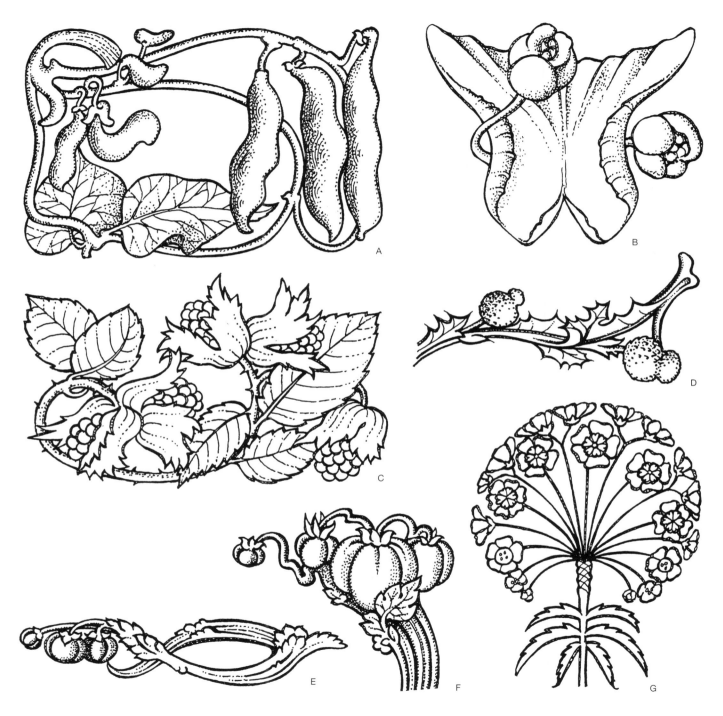

A

B

C

D

E

F

G

A

B

C

D

E

F

G

H

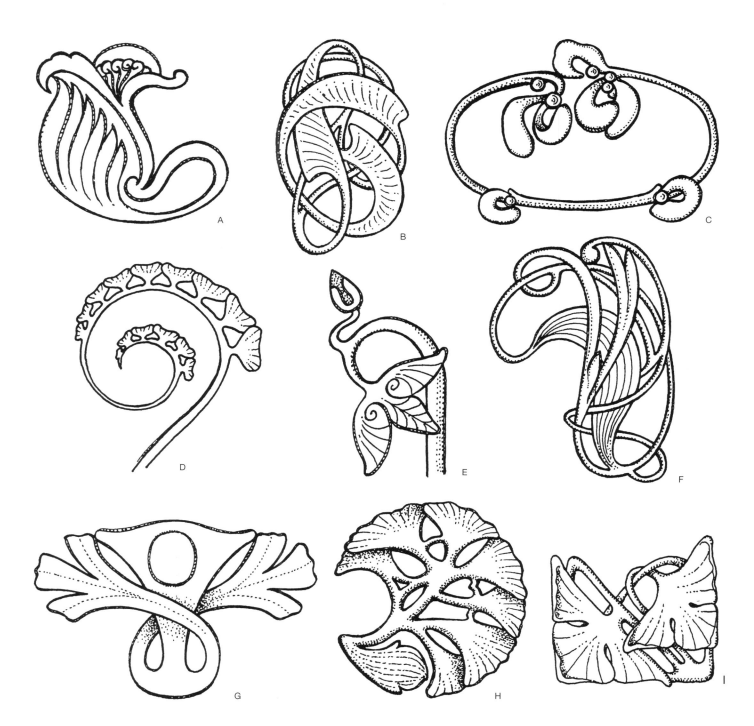

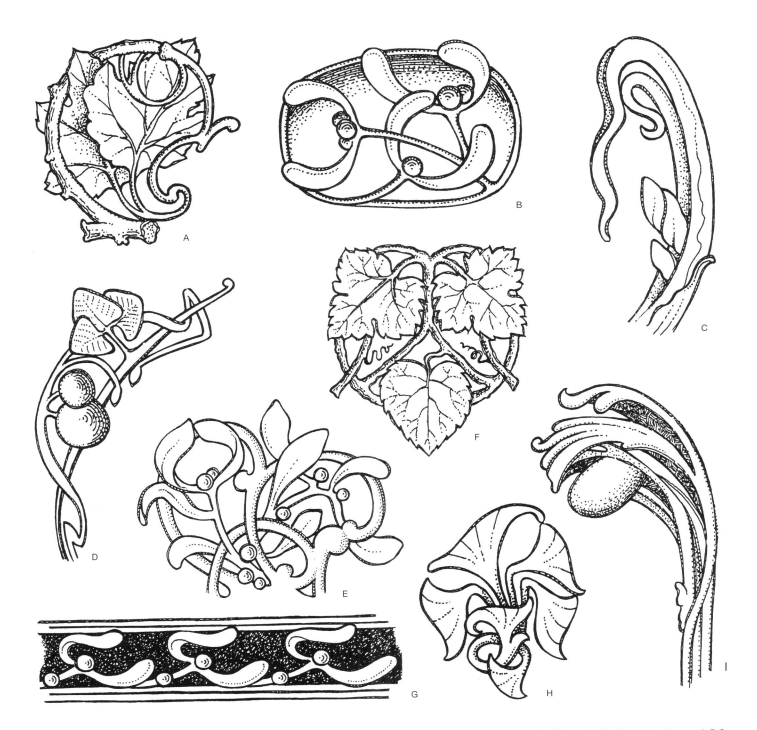

A

B

C

D

E

F

G

H

I

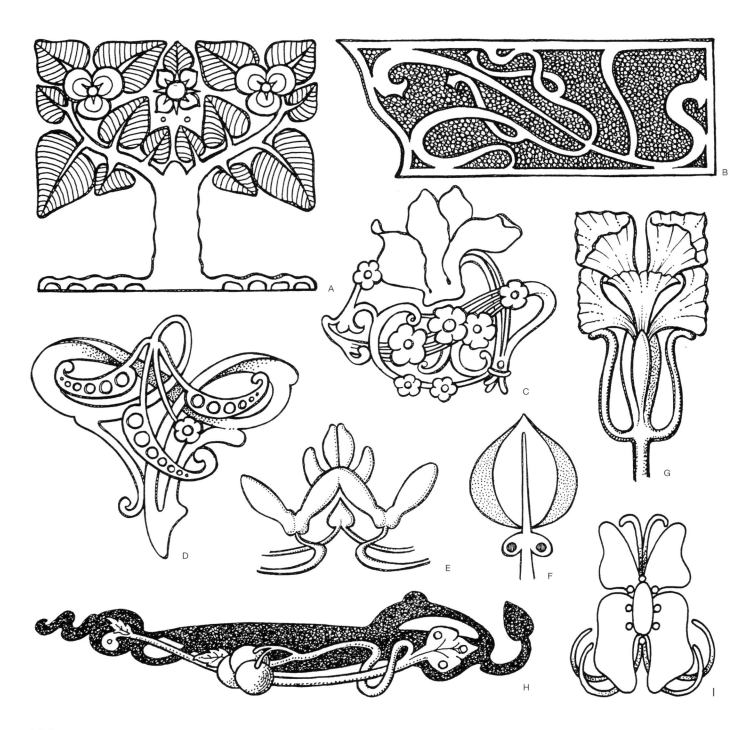

A

B

C

D

E

F

G

H

I

A

B

C

D

A

B

C

D

E

F

G

H

ART DECO

A

B

C

D

E

F

G

H

I

J

K

L

M

N

O

P

Q

R

S

A

B

C

D

E

F

G

H

I

J

K

L

M

N

O

P

Q

R

S

A   B   C   D   E   F   G   H   I   J   K

A

B

C

D

E

F

G

H

A B C D E F G H I

A

B

C

D

E

A

B

C

D

E

F

G

H

I

A

B

C

D

E

F

G

H

I

J

K

FLOWERS

A

B

C

D

E

F

G

H

I

J

K

L

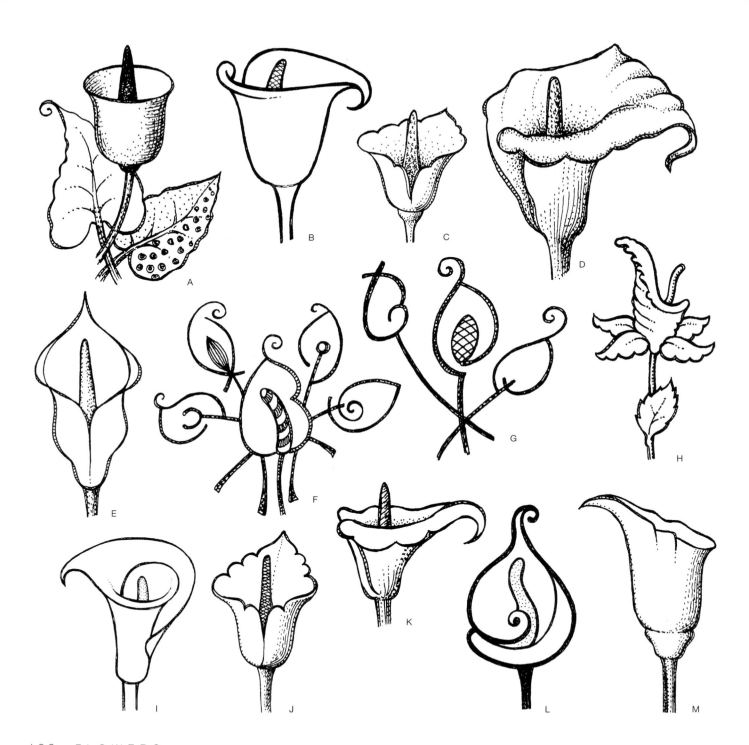

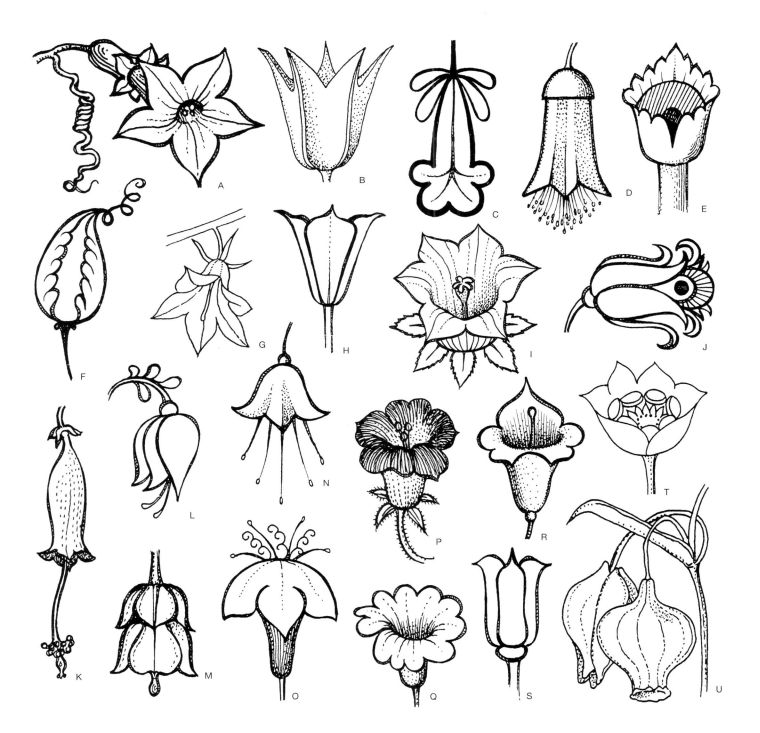

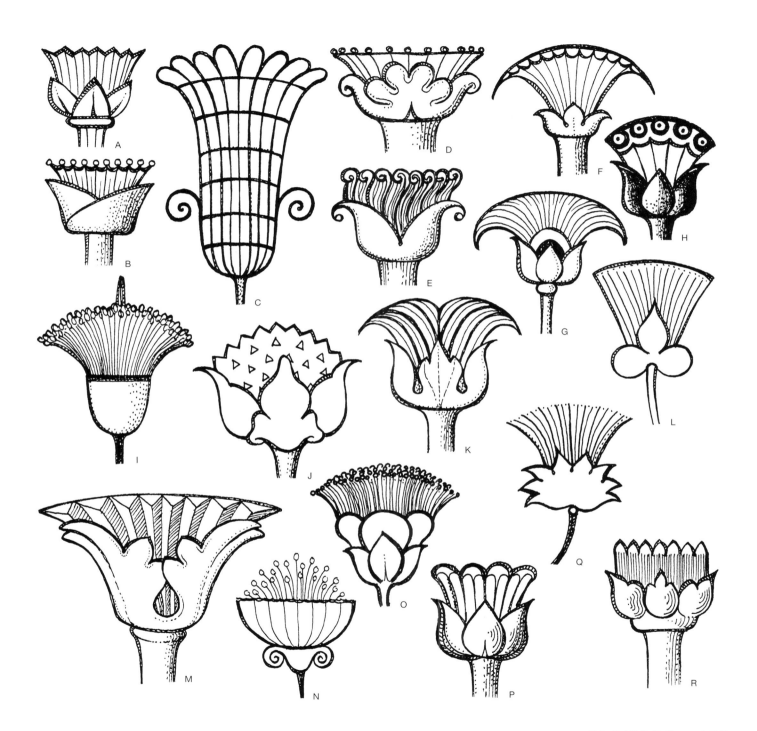

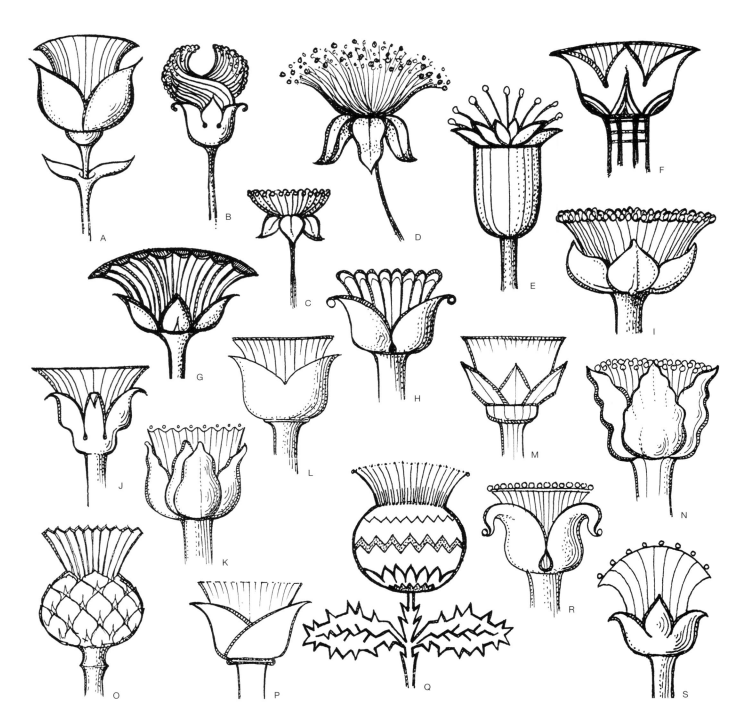

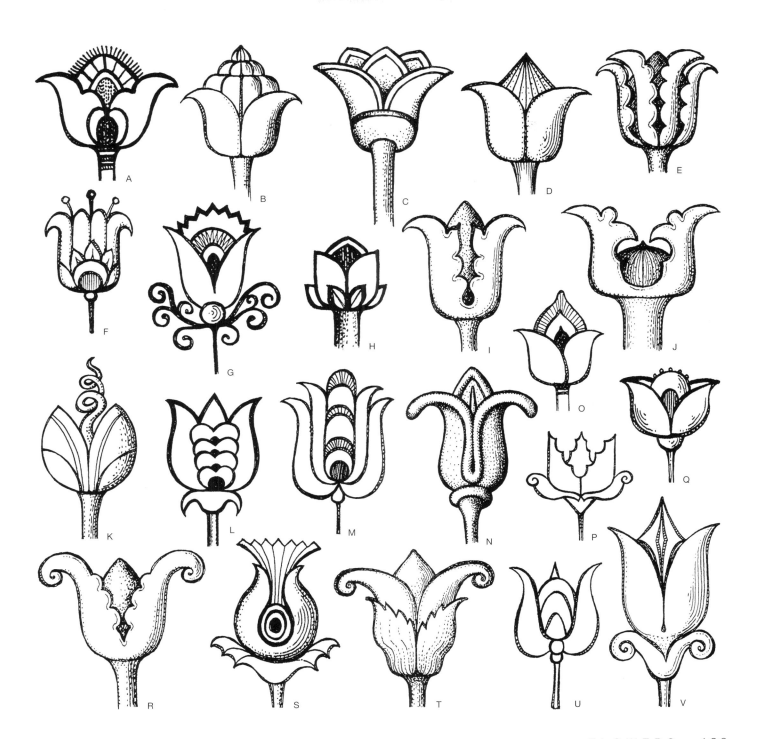

A B C D E F G H I J K L M N O

A

B

C

D

E

F

G

H

I

J

A

B

C

D

E

H

F

G

I

A

B

C

D

E

F

G

H

I

J

K

L

M

N

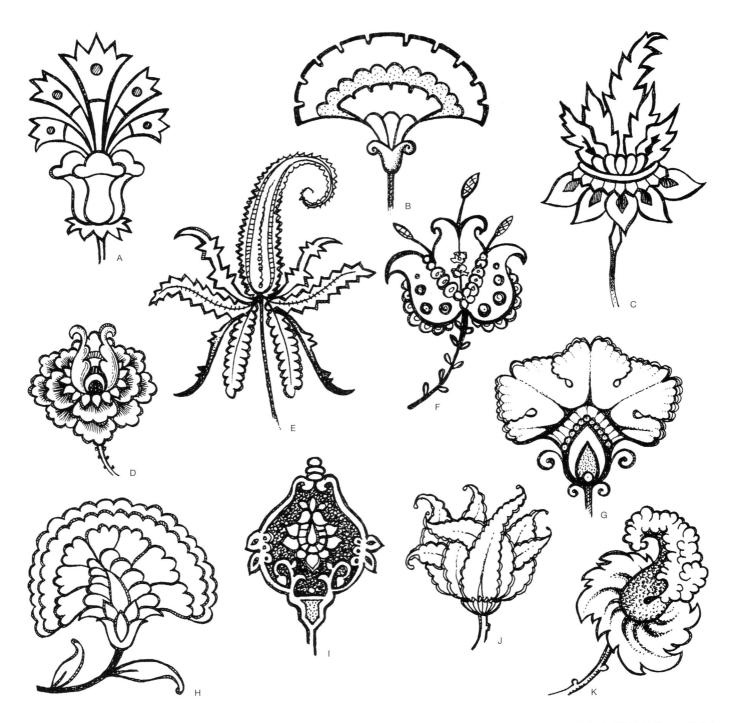

A

B

C

D

E

F

G

H

I

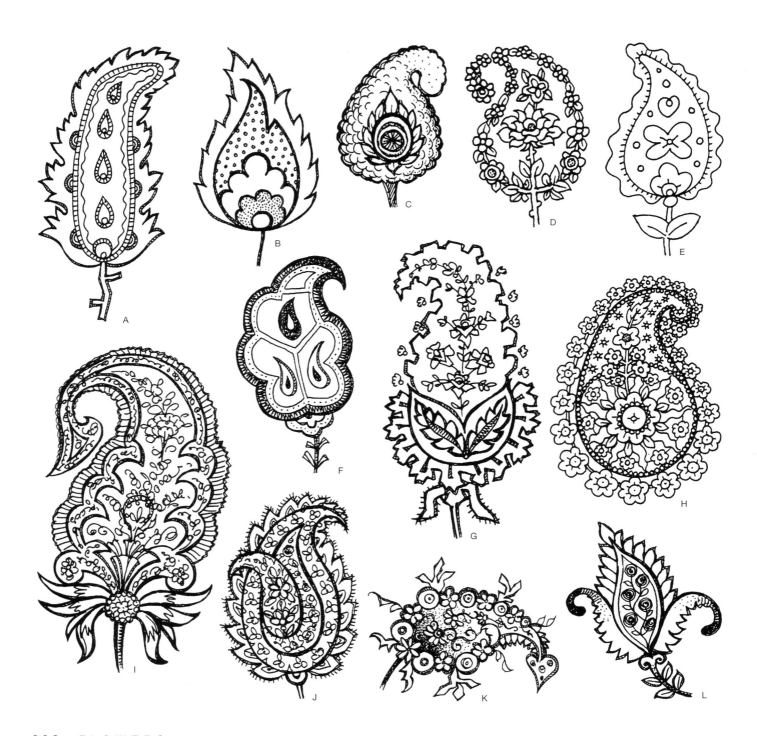

A

B

C

D

E

F

G

H

I

J

K

L

A B C D E F G H I J K L M N O P Q R S T

A B C D E F G H

A

B

C

D

E

F

G

H

I

J

K

L

M

N

O

P

Q

R

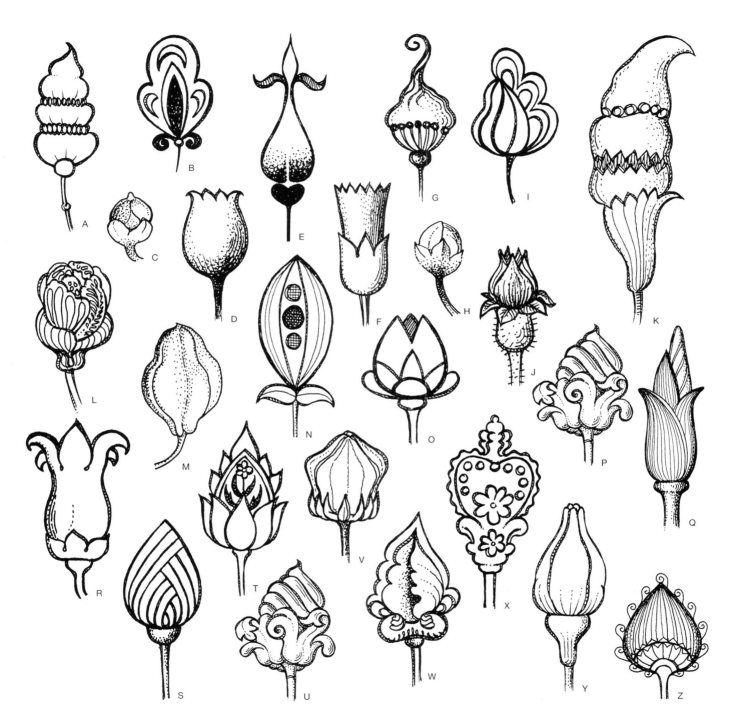

A
B
C
D
E
F
G
H
I
J
K
L
M
N
O
P
Q
R
S
T
U
V
W
X
Y
Z

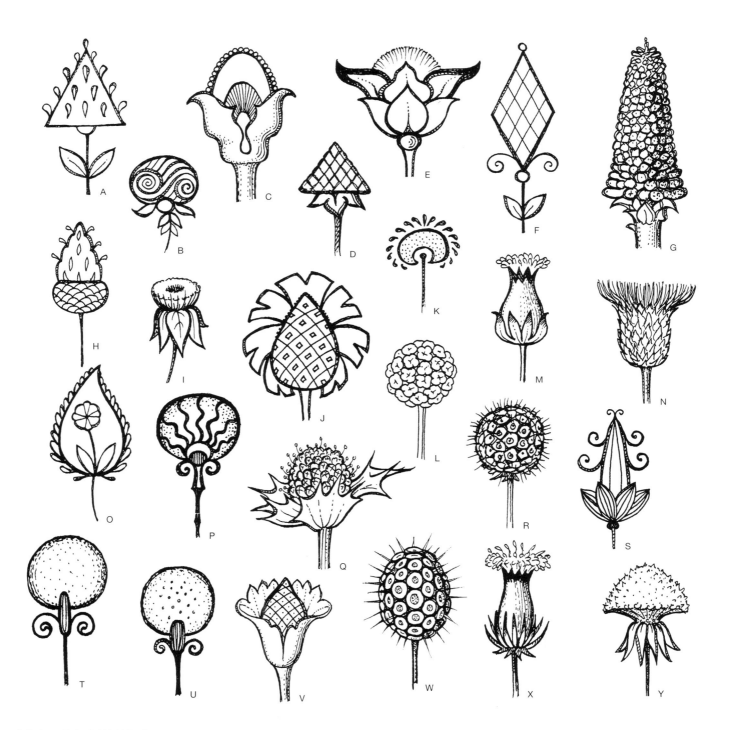

A

B

C

D

F

E

G

H

I

J

K

LEAVES

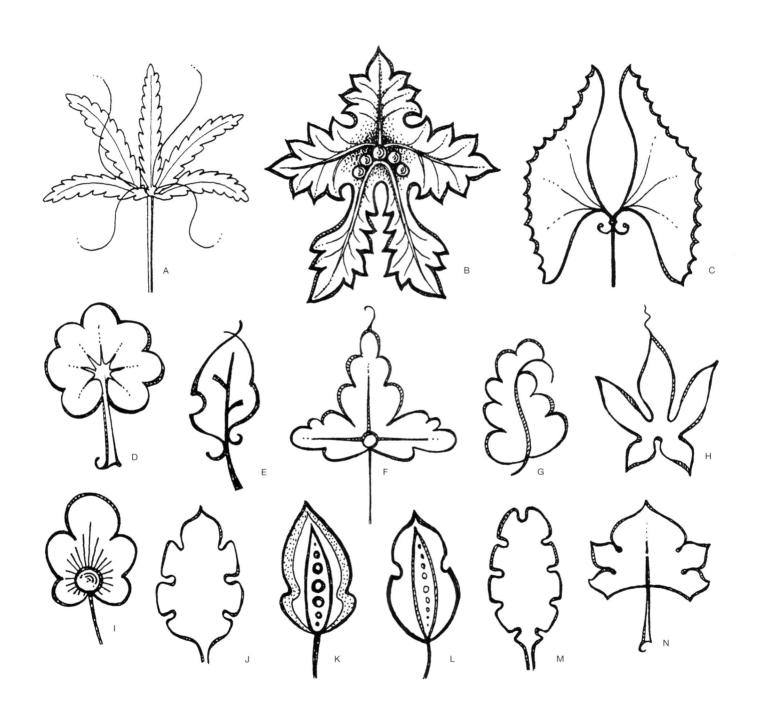

A   B   C

D   E   F   G   H

I   J   K   L   M   N

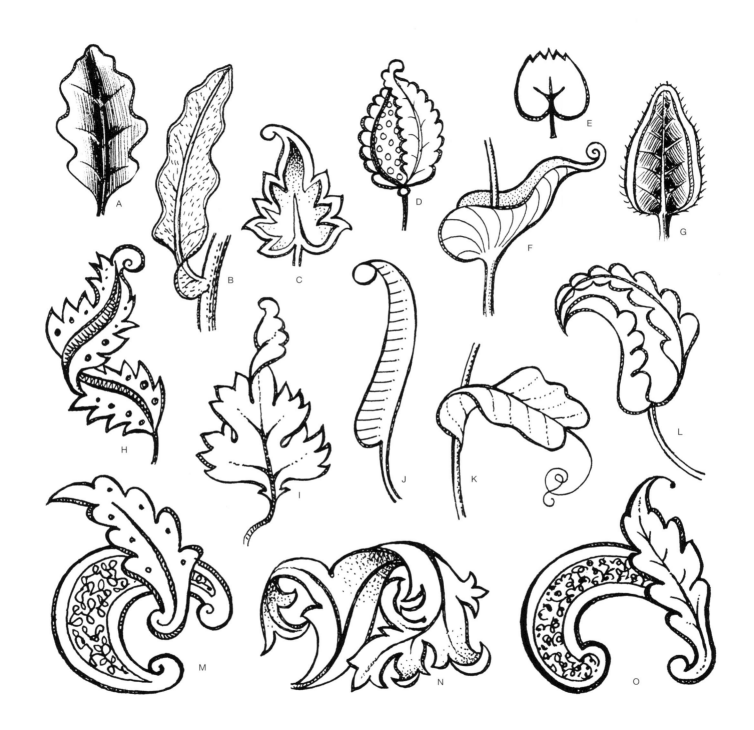

A

B

C

D

E

F

G

H

I

J

K

L

M

N

O

P

Q

R

S

T

U

V

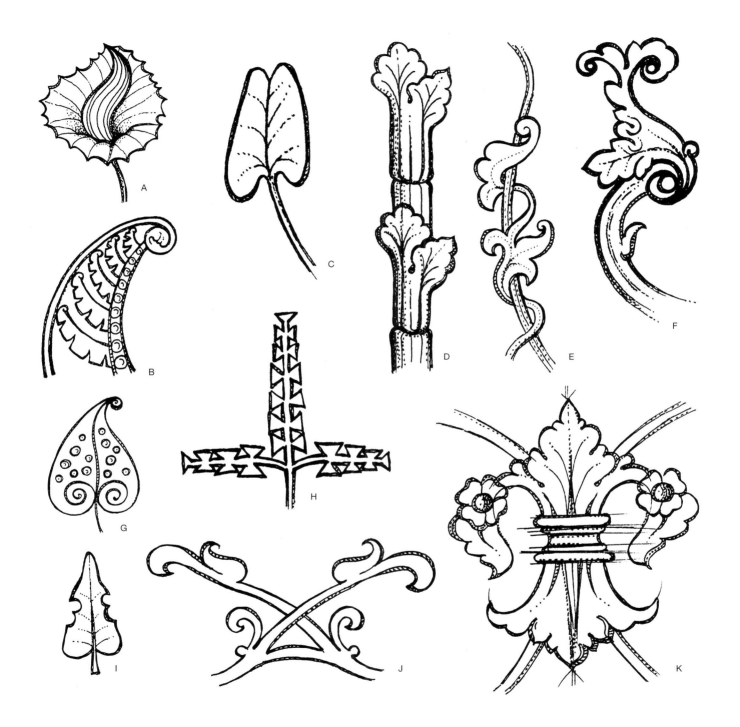

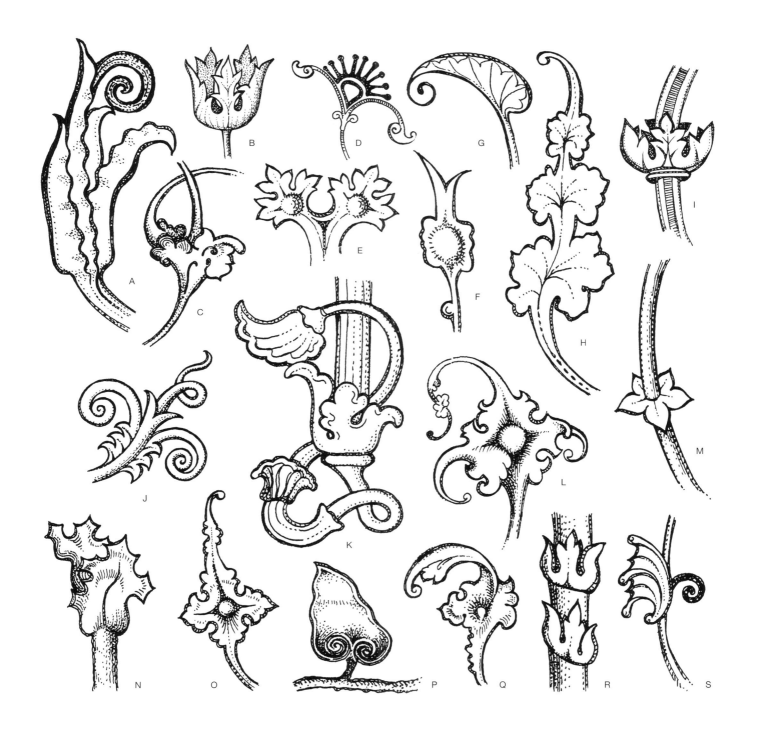

FRUIT

A   B   C   D

E   F   G   H

I   J   K   L

A

B

C

D

E

F

G

H

I

J

K

L

M

A

B

C

D

E

F

G

H

I

J

K

L

A

B

C

D

E

F

G

H

I

J

K

L

M

N

O

P

A

B

C

D

E

F

G

H

I

J

K

L

M

N

O

P

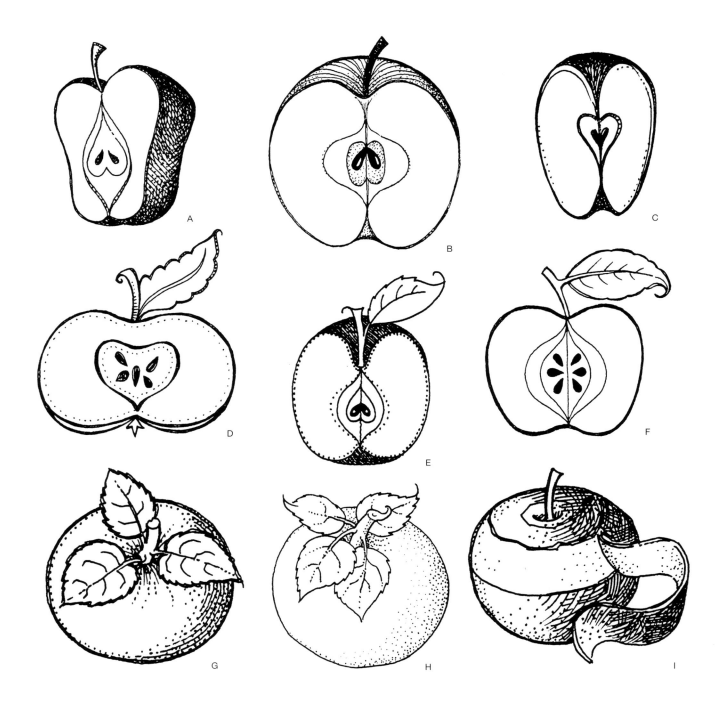

A

B

C

D

E

F

G

H

I

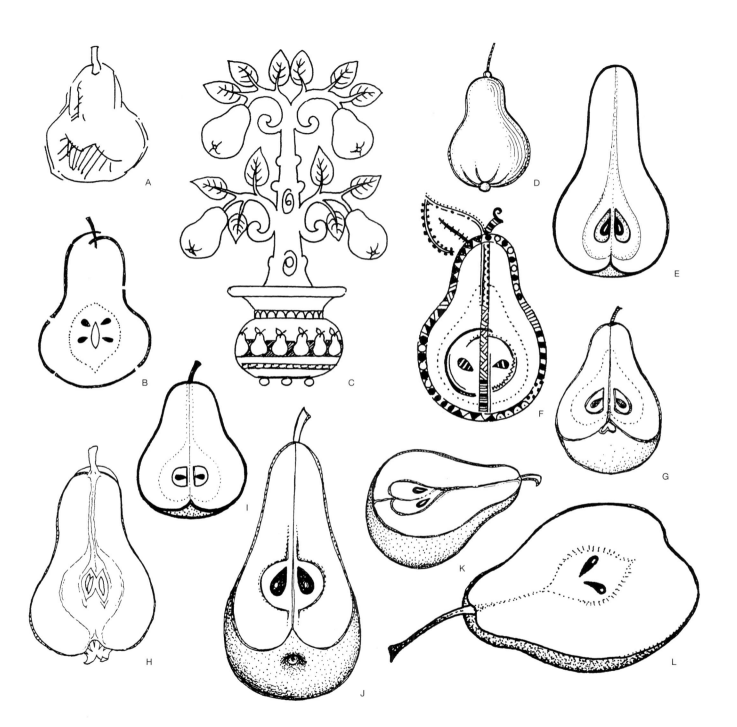

A

B

C

D

E

F

G

H

I

J

K

L

A

B

C

D

E

F

G

H

I

J

K

L

M

A

B

C

D

E

F

G

H

I

J

K

L

A

B

C

D

E

E

F

G

H

A

B

C

D

E

F

A   B   C   D   E   F   G   H   I   J   K   L

A B C D E

F G H I J

K L M N

A

B

C

D

E

F

G

H

I

J

K

L

M

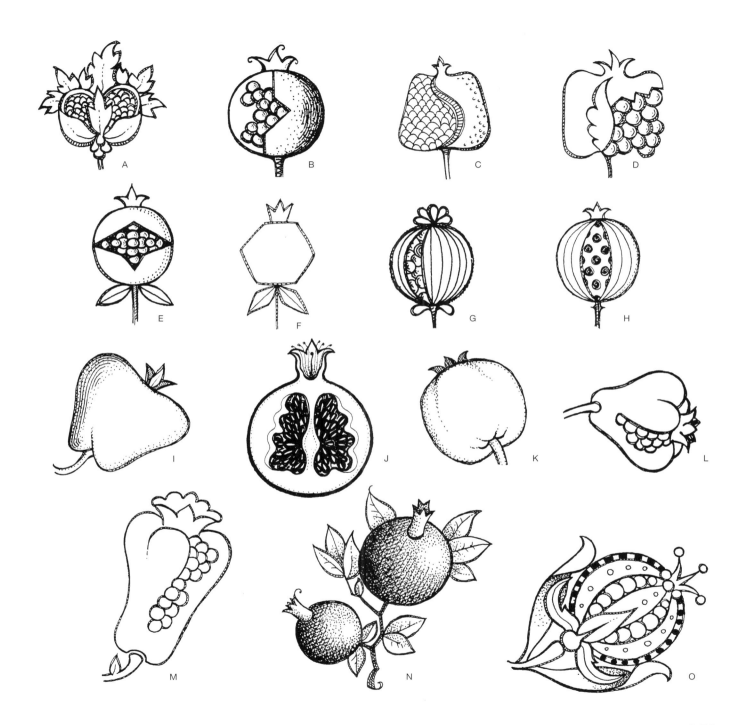

A

B

C

D

E

F

G

H

I

J

K

L

M

N

O

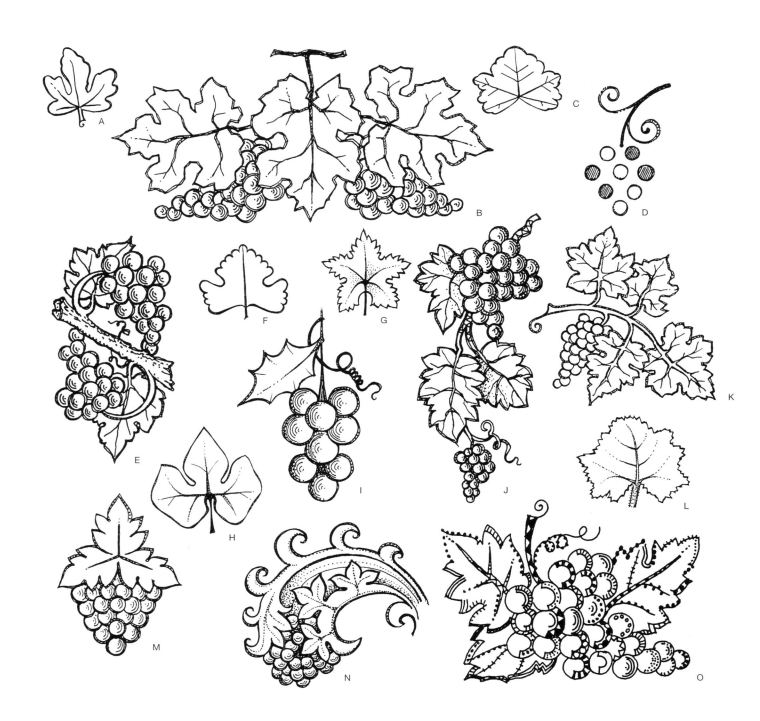

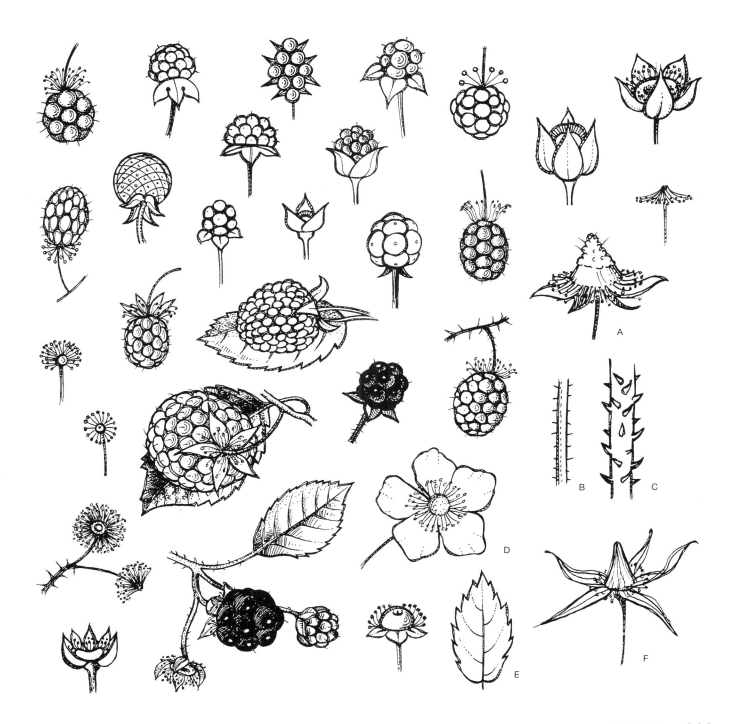

A

B

C

D

E

F

G

H

I

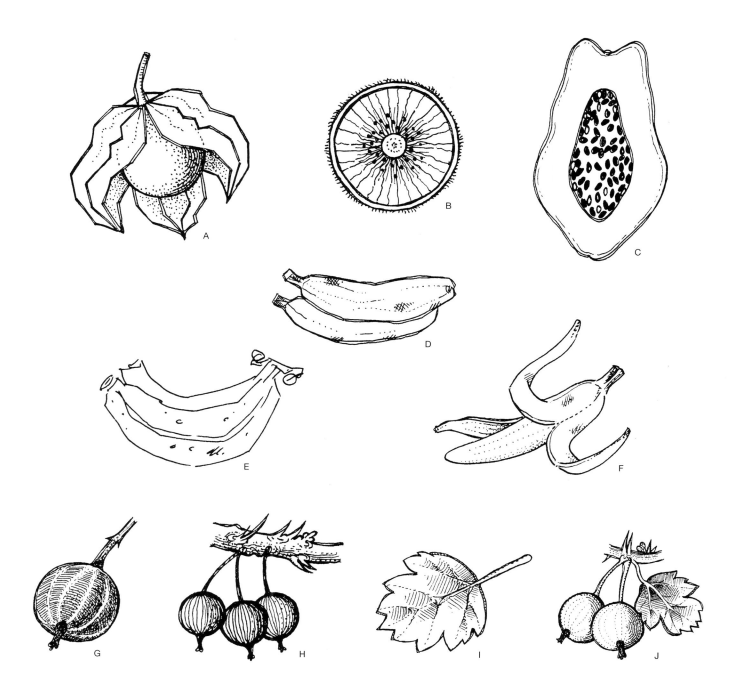

VEGETABLES

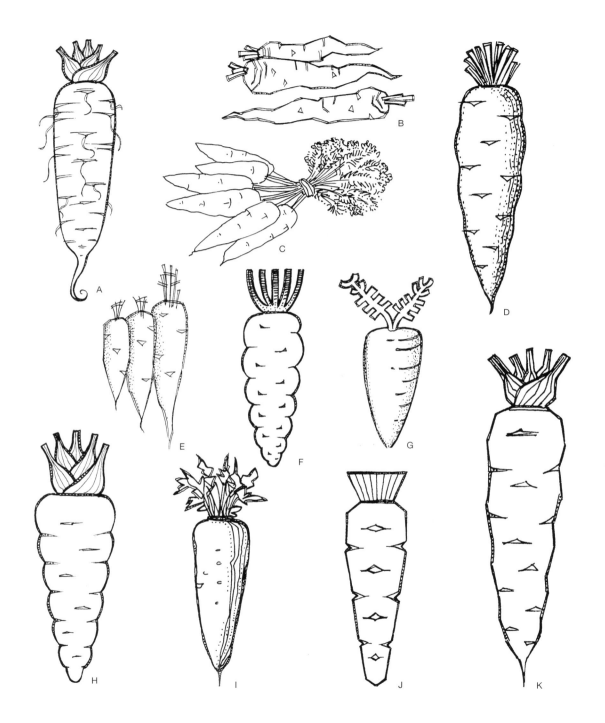

A

B

C

D

E

F

G

H

I

J

K

L

M

A

B

C

D

E

F

G

H

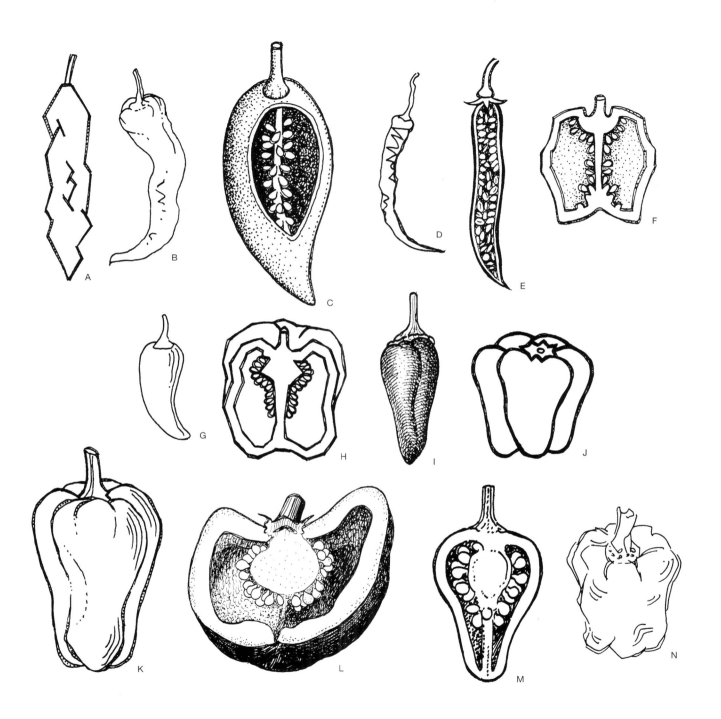

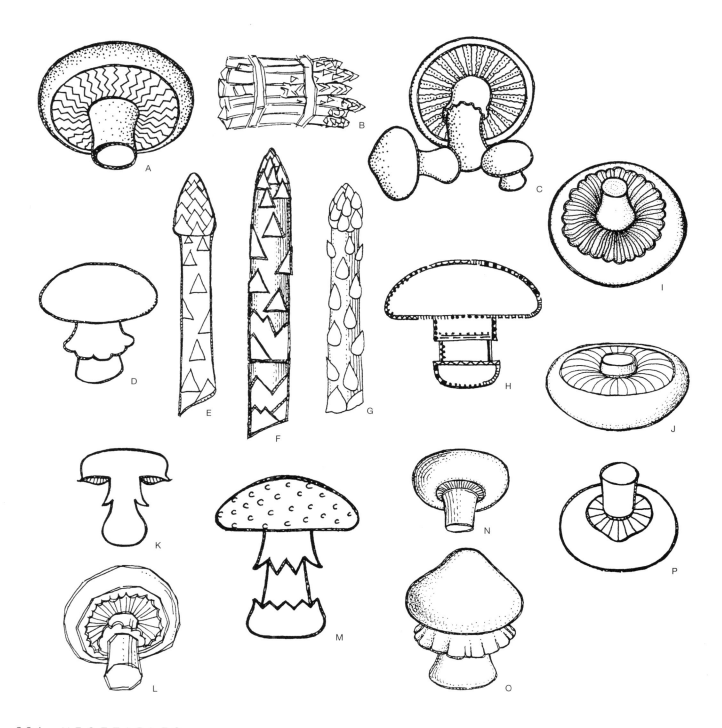

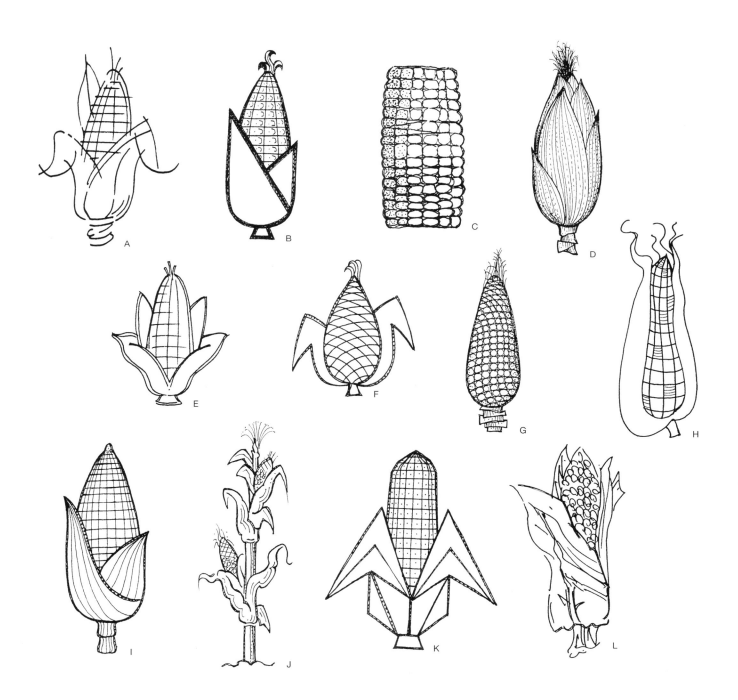

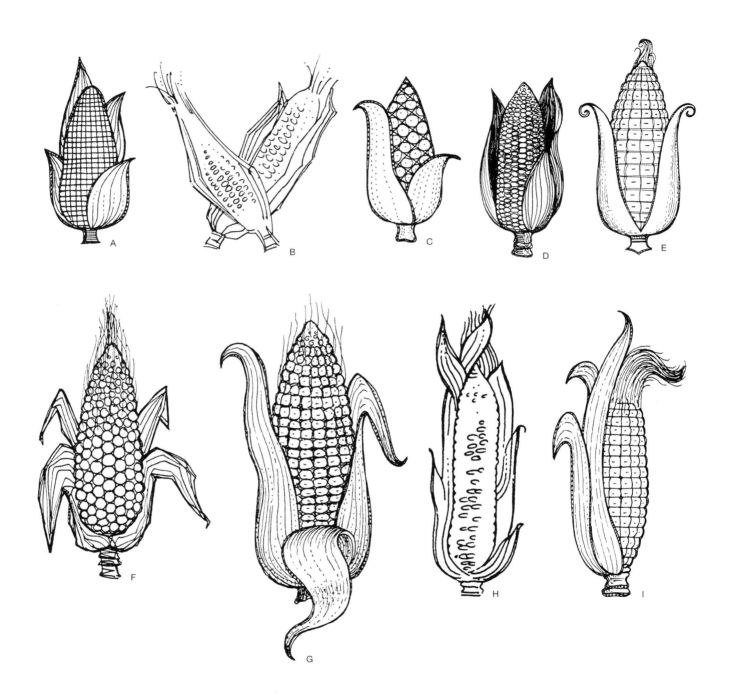

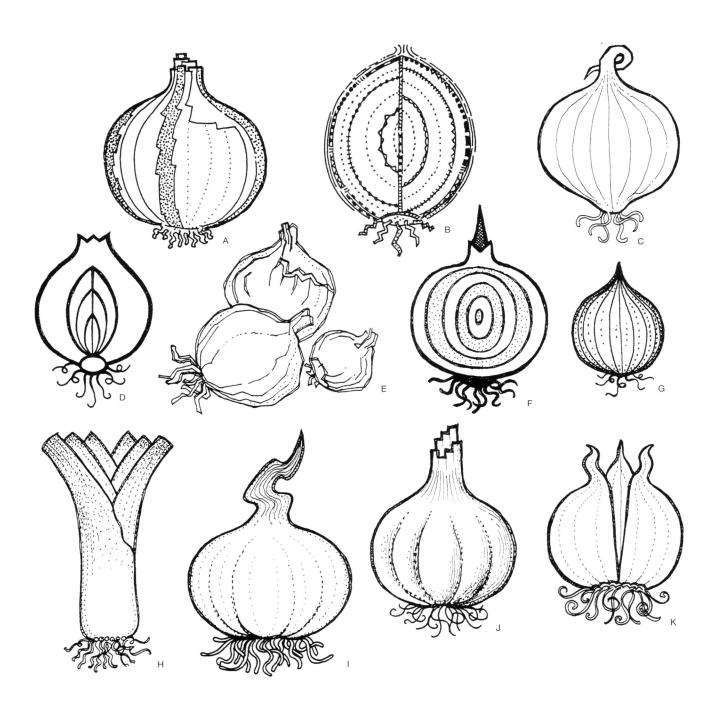

A

B

C

D

E

F

G

H

I

J

K

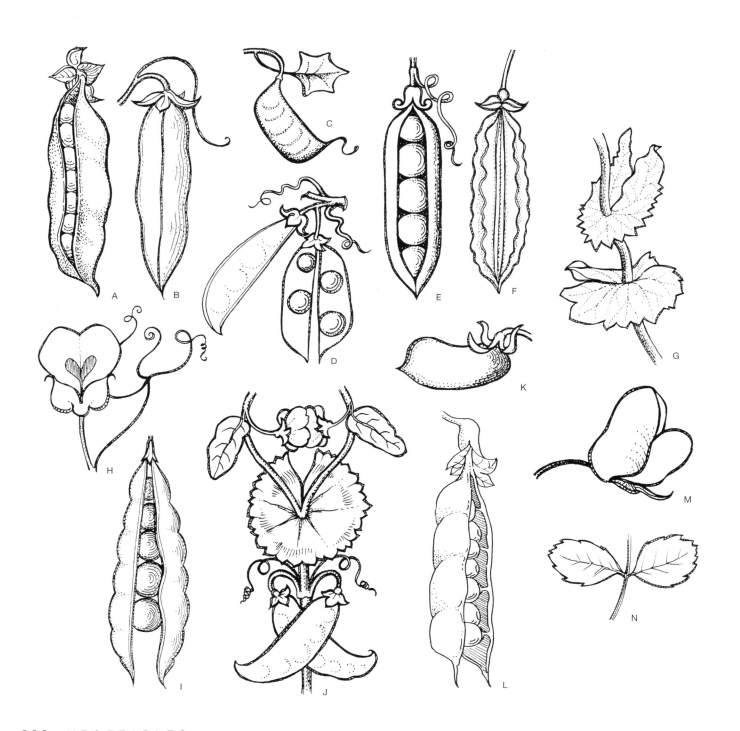

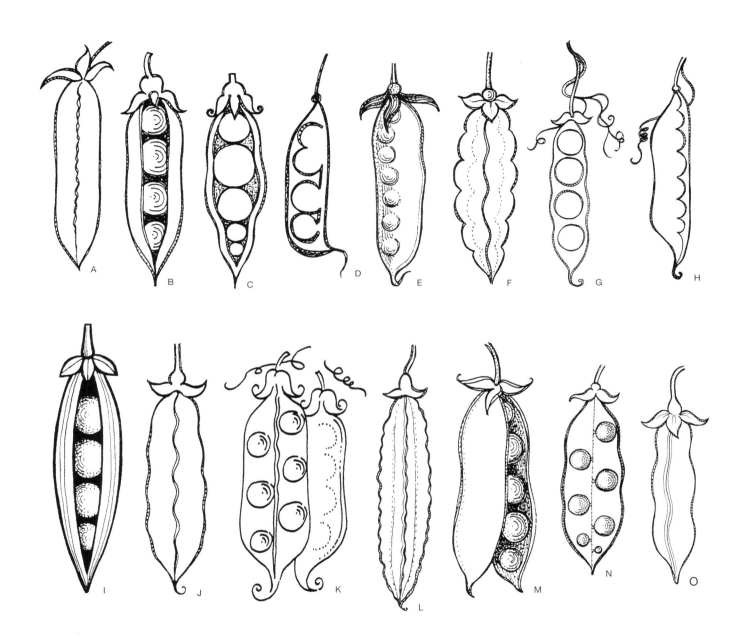

A   B   C   D   E   F   G   H

I   J   K   L   M   N   O

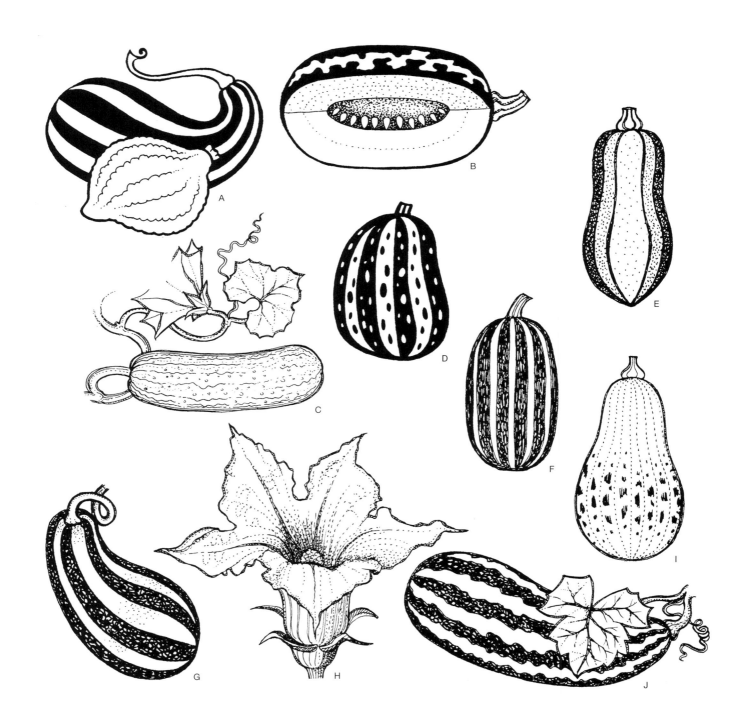

A

B

C

D

E

F

G

H

I

J

K

L

M

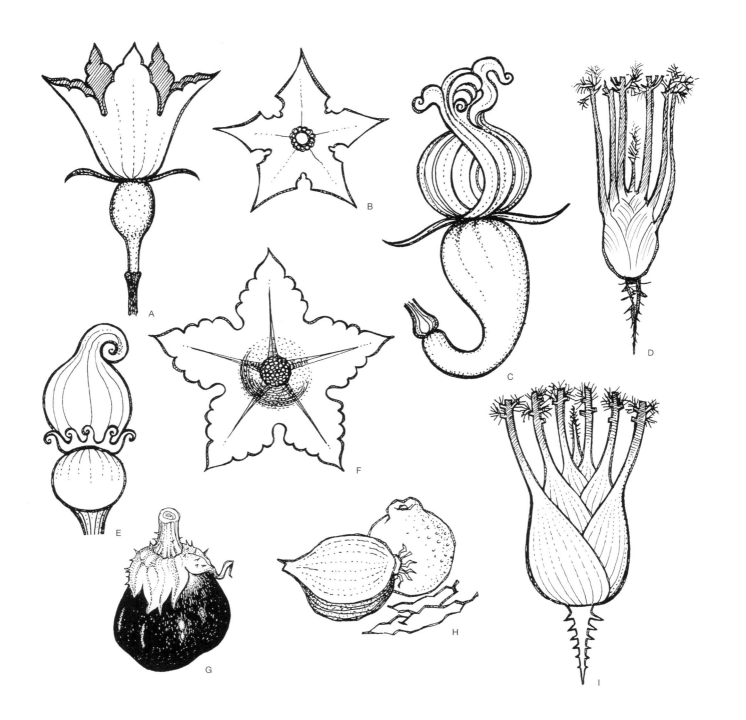

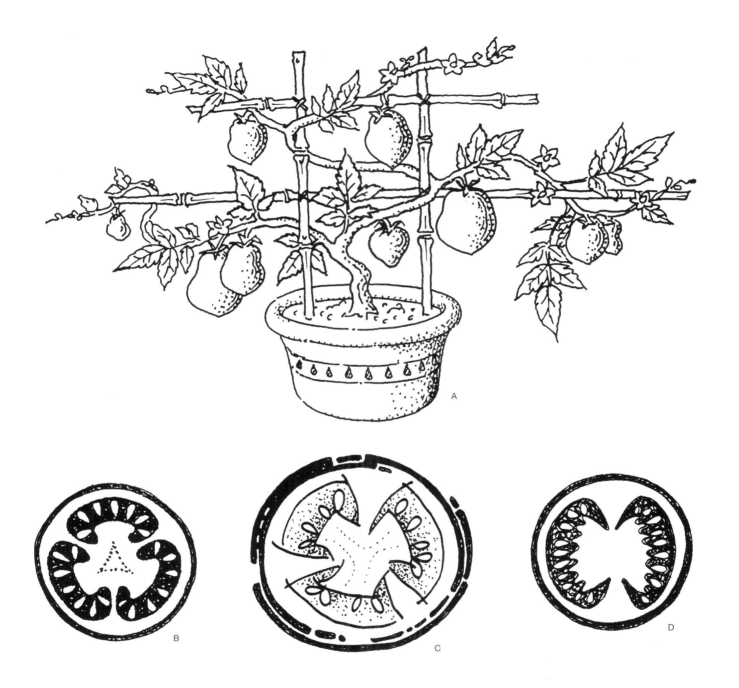

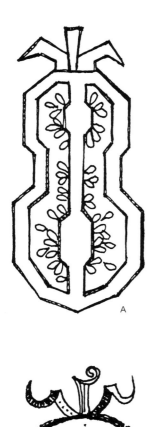

A

B

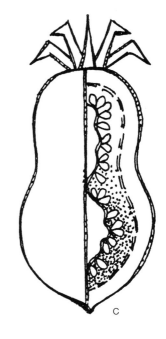

C

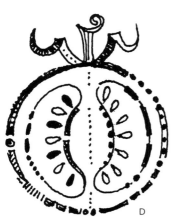

D

E

F

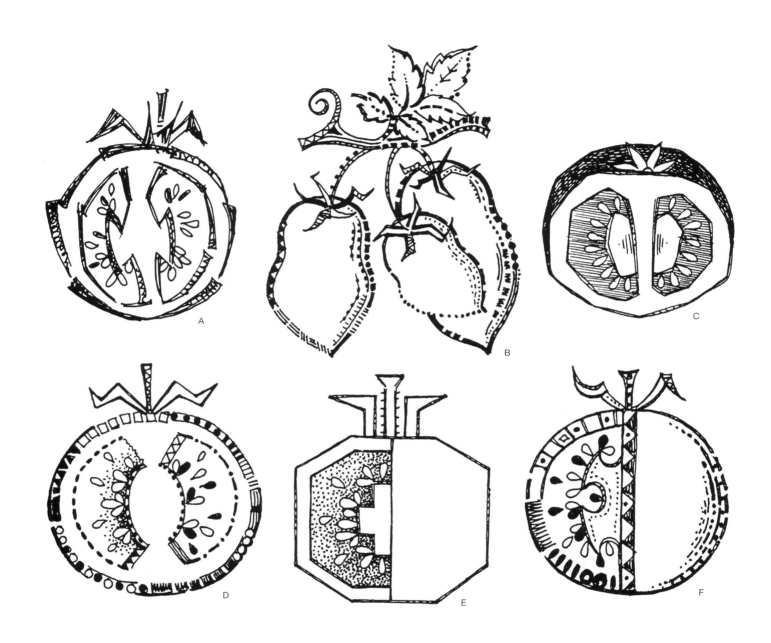

A

B

C

D

E

F

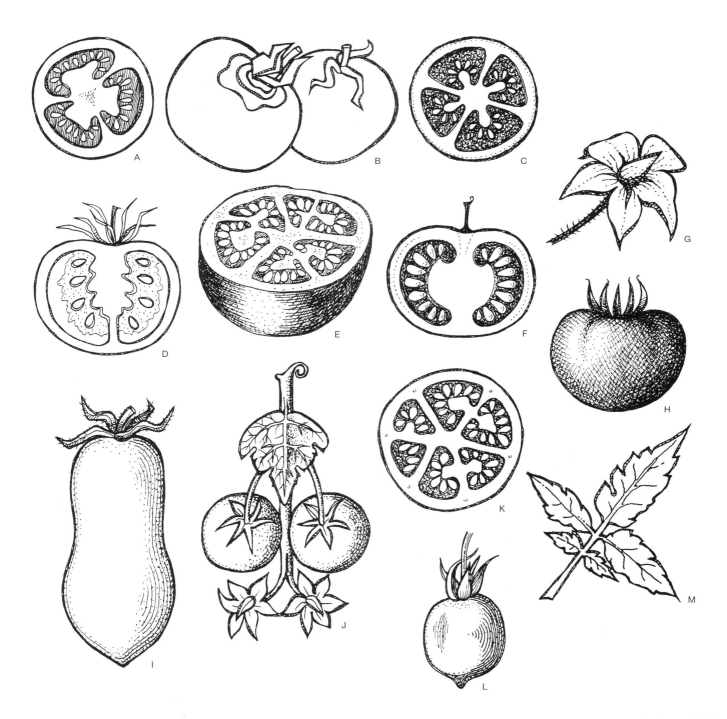

A

B

C

D

E

F

G

H

I

J

K

L

M

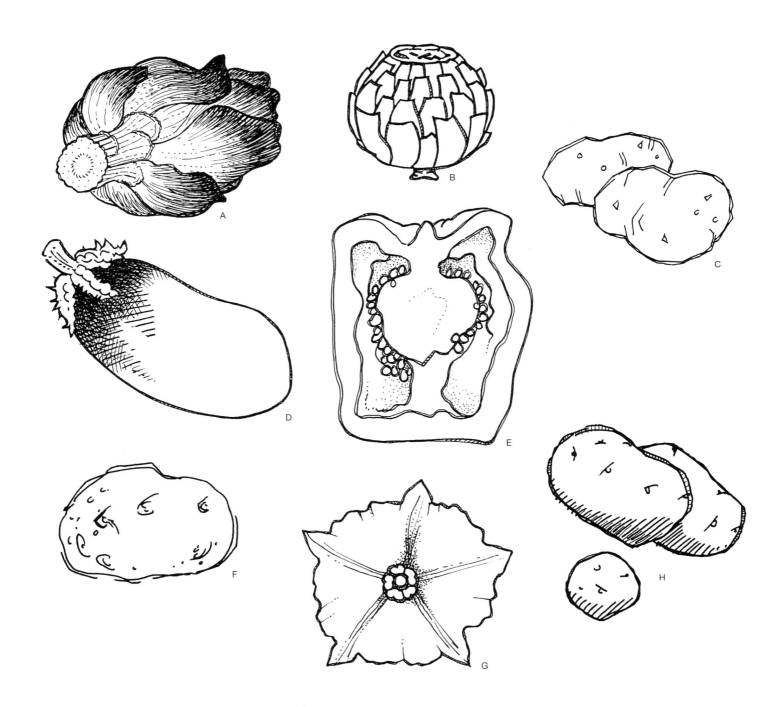

FRUITING BODIES

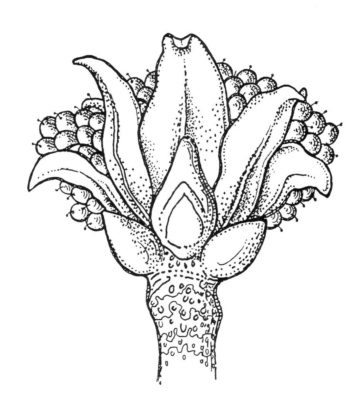

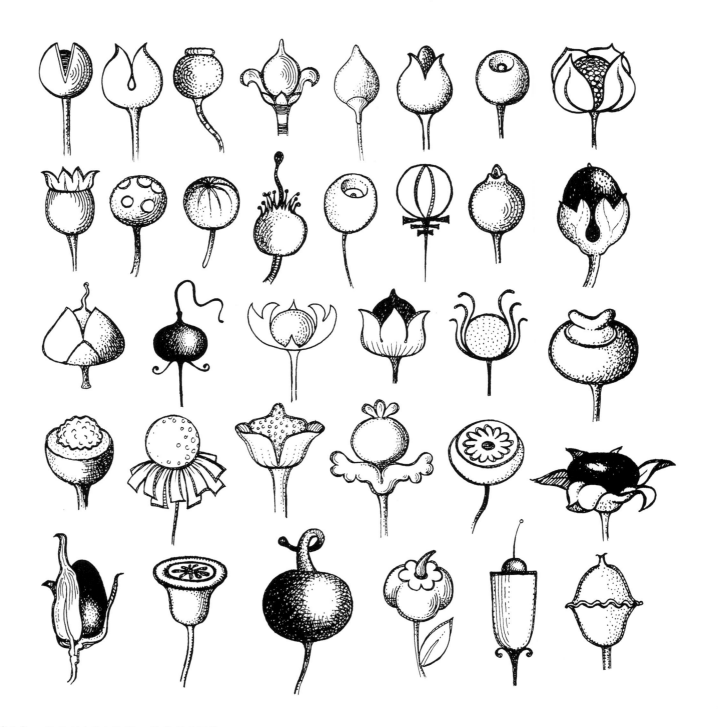

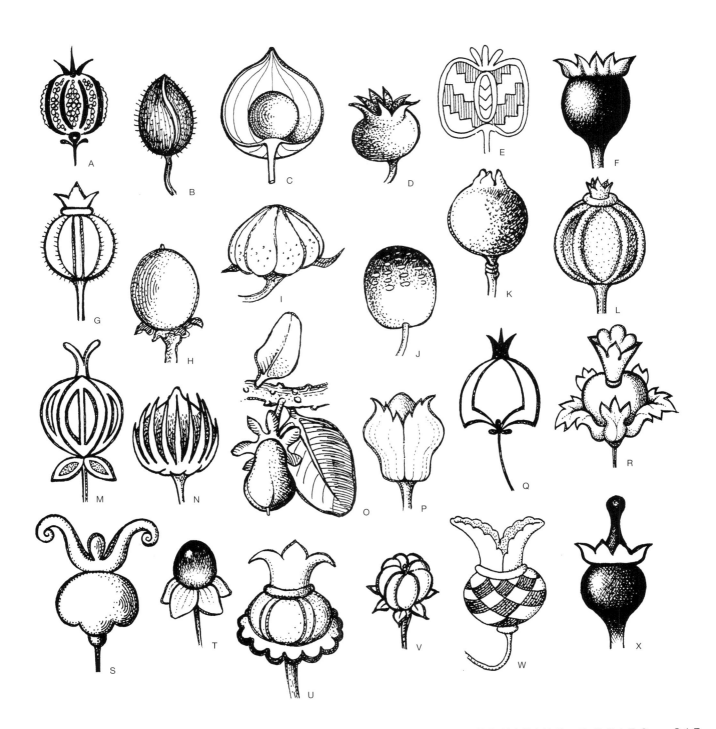

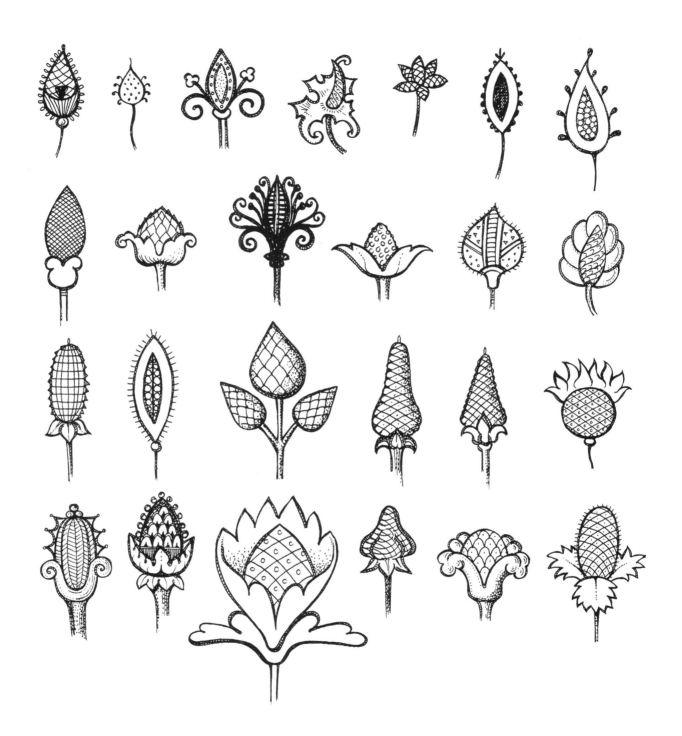

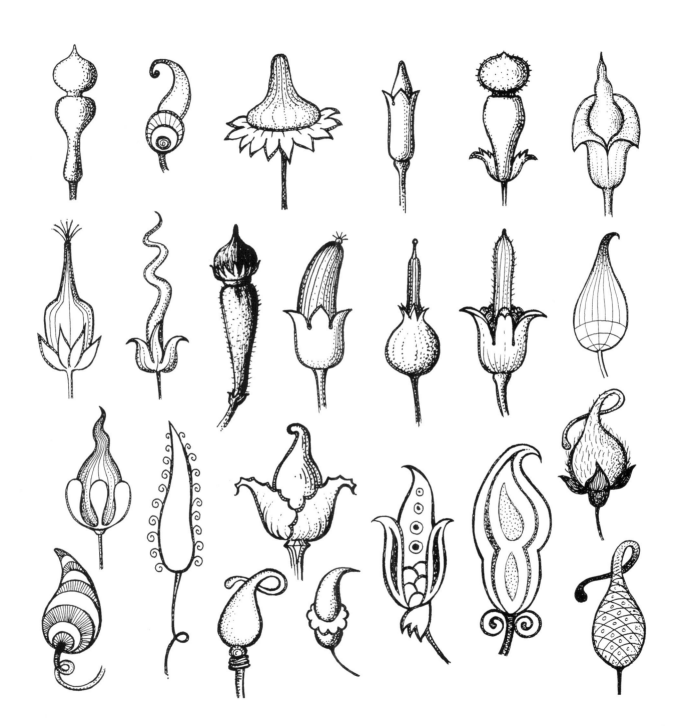

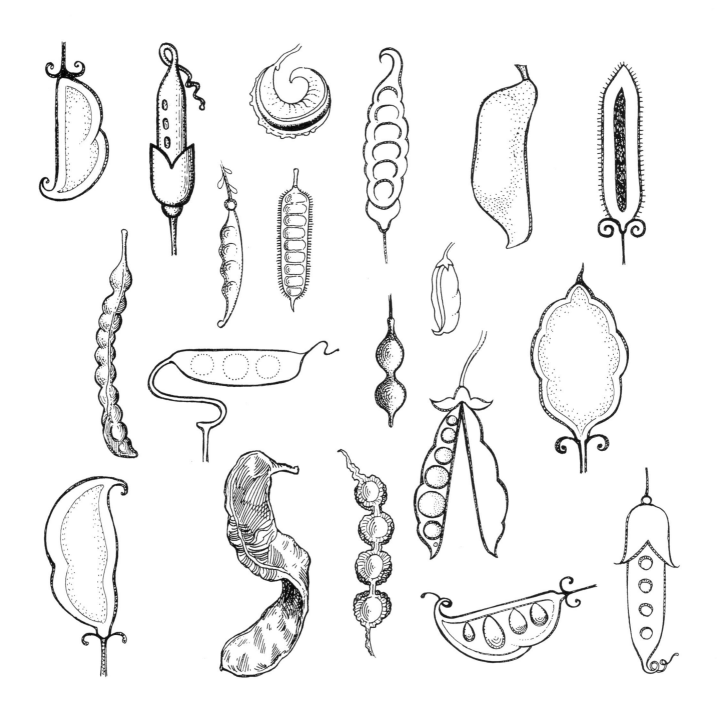

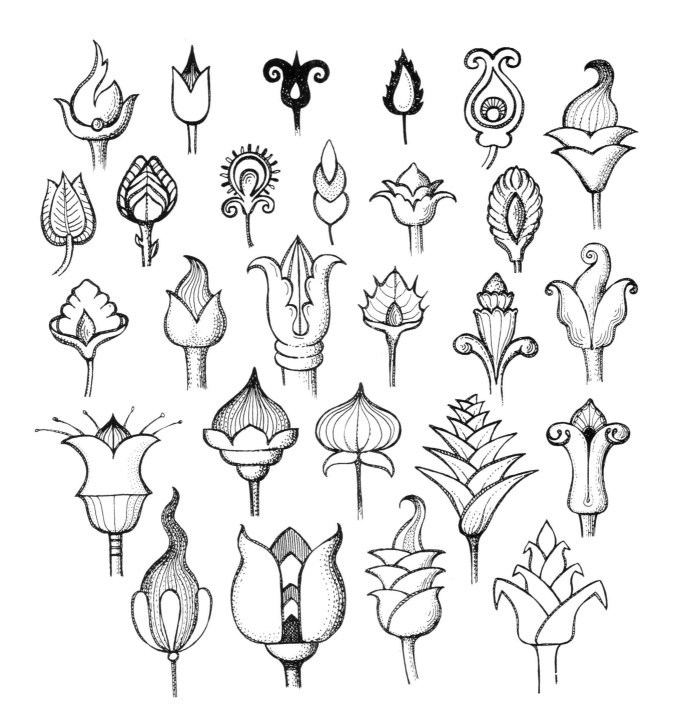

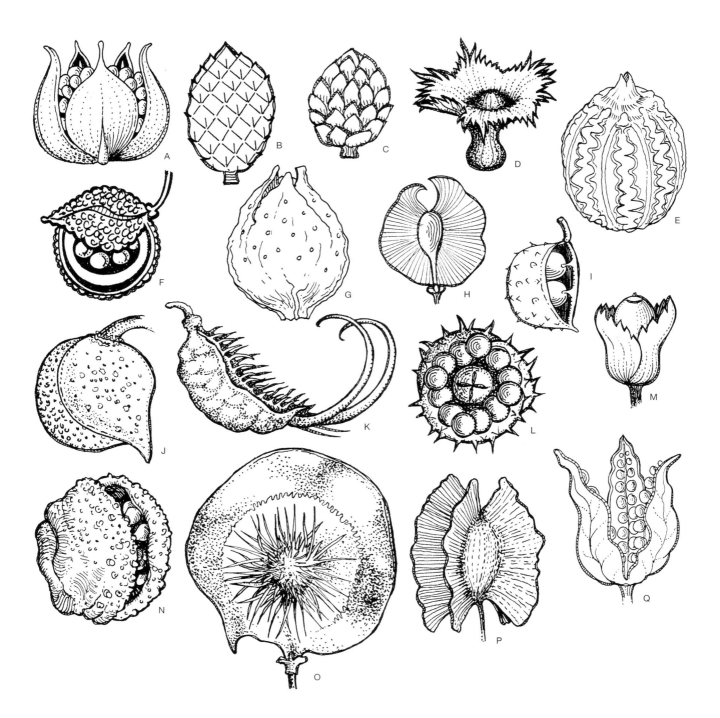

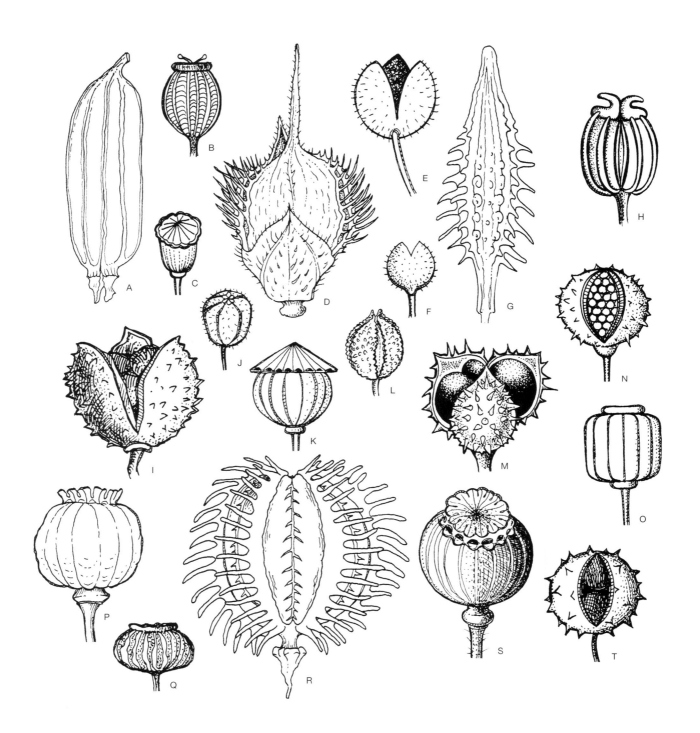

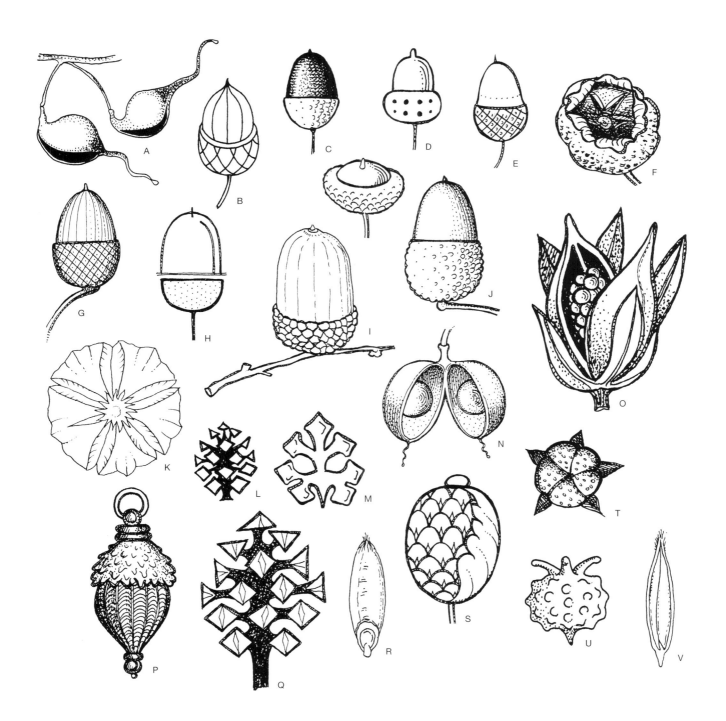

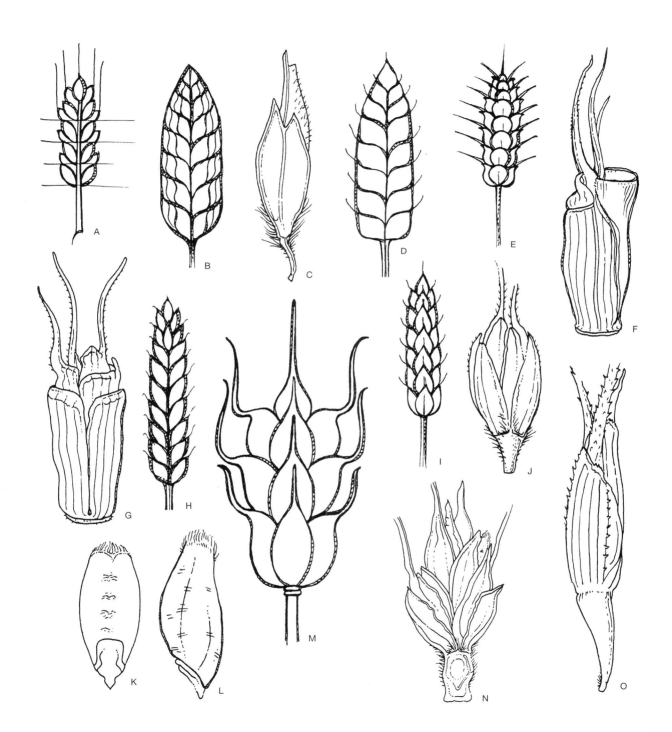

TREES

A

B

C

D

E

F

G

H

A

B

C

D

E

F

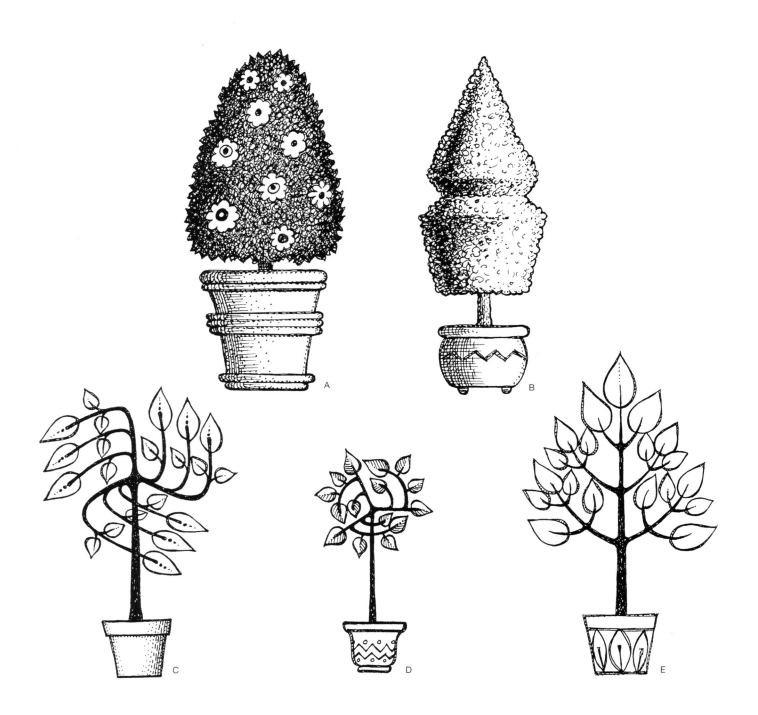

A

B

C

D

E

F

A

B

C

D

E

F

G

H

A

B

C

D

E

F

A

B

C

D

E

F

MOTIFS

A

B

C

D

E

F

G

H

I

J

K

L

A

B

C

D

E

F

G

A

B

C

D

E

F

G

H

I

J

K

L

M

N

O

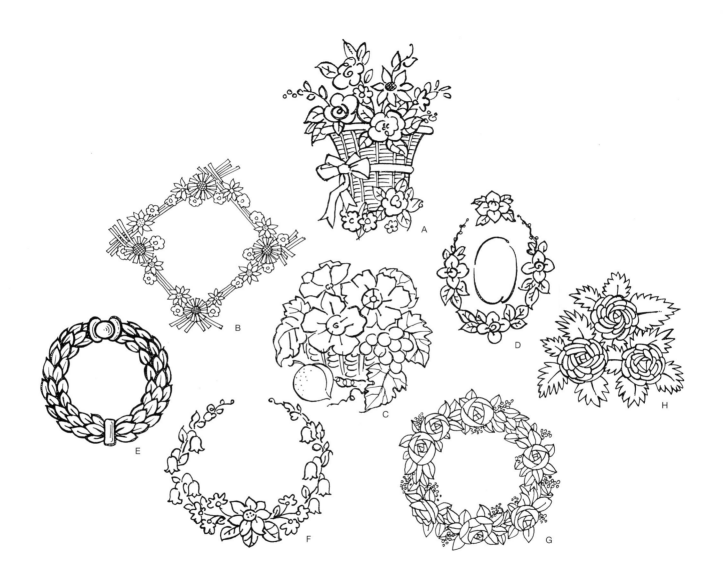

A

B

C

D

E

F

G

A

B

C

D

E

F

G

H

I

J

K

L

M

N

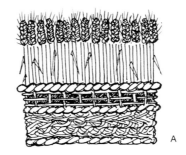

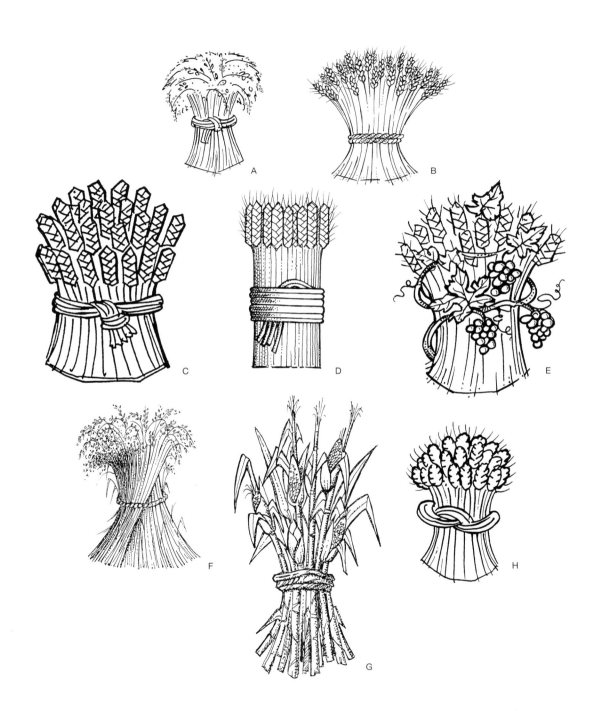

A

B

C

D

E

F

G

H

BORDERS

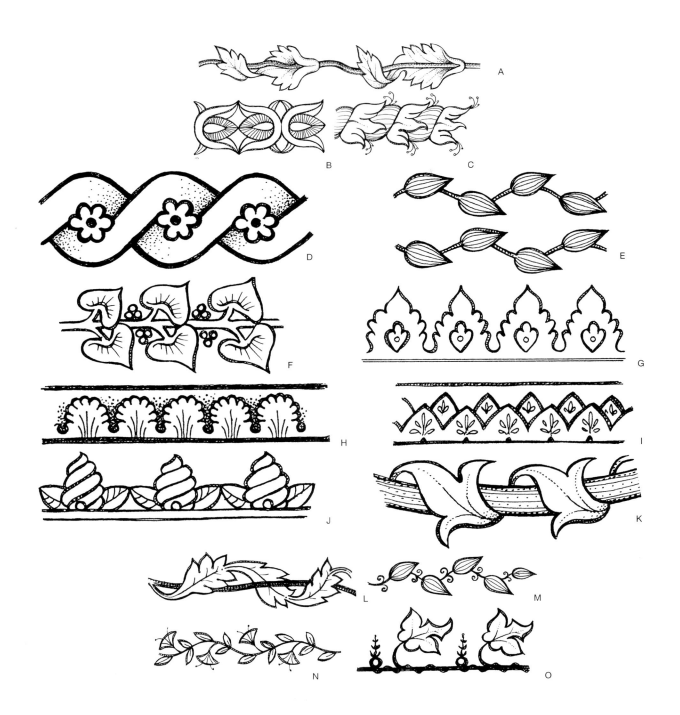

A

B

C

D

E

F

G

H

I

J

K

L

M

N

O

INDEX

Acanthus		42 BCDFGHIKL
Acanthus	Border	39, 43 A,47 AEGKMN, 48 CFGK, 49 AIJ, 50 CDEFJK,52 H,56 E,73 ACFKL, 74 BEH, 372 T, 373AHKL, 374 MRS,375 F
Acanthus	Cresting	60 GPQ
Acanthus	Finial	60 DGMNOP, 249 I
Acanthus	Flower	32 BK
Acanthus	Leaf	32 BKM, 41 ABCDEGJ, 42 CDGKL, 44, 47 AEGKMN, 48 CFGK, 49 AIJ, 50 CDEFJK, 53 B, 56 E, 60 ADEGHIJKLM NOPQST, 61, 66 BCFGJKLNR, 67 BIJR TU, 73 ACFKL, 74 BEH, 82 BDEIK, 244 HIMNO, 248 E, 249 AFIS, 251 L, 252 E, 253 DEFK, 254 BCEFGKL, 255 ABCDE FGHIJKLMNOPQRS
Acanthus	Motif	40 ABCHKL, 41 DF, 43 FGHIL, 53 B, 66 BCFGJRTU, 67 BIJRTU, 82 I, 244 MNO, 253 K
Acanthus	Rosette	53 B
Acanthus	Seed	42 FI
Acanthus	Stem	32 M, 33 M, 60 EJST, 255 CIJKMNR
Acorn		346 AEFI
Acorn	Motif	59 B
Acorns	Capsule	327 BCDEGHIJ
Acorns	Oak	247 A
Agapanthus	Motif	366 A
Allium	Motif	151 D
Anthemion	Border	36 ABGKL, 37 ABCEG
Anthemion	Design	31, 33 ABCDEFGIJ, 35 BE, 36 ABGKL, 37 ABCEG, 38 ACD
Anthurium	Motif	144 A
Apple	Cross-Section	262 ADEIJKMO, 263 ABCDEGIMOL, 264 ABDF
Apple	Folk-like	262 CDEFKMO, 263 ABCEFI, 264 DF
Apple	Leaf	262 NP, 263 H, 264 EFGH
Apple	Motif	95 B, 113 B, 136 E, 262 ABCDE FGHIJKLMNOP, 263 ABCDE FGHIJKLMNOP, 264 ABCDE FGHI, 351, 370 C
Apple	Peeled	264 I
Apple	Quartered	262 GH, 263 N, 264 CE
Apple	Seed	262 AEGIJ
Apple	Sprig	262 BFN, 263 H
Apple	Tree	71 AG, 335 CDEG, 347 B, 348 AD
Apple Tree	Folk-like	336 C
Apple Tree	Motif	71 AG, 335 CDEG, 336 ACDE
Arabesque	Design	83, 84, 85
Arabesque	Leaf	83, 84, 85
Arabesque	Tree	88

Arrowhead	Motif	150 E
Artichoke	Motif	308 AB
Arum Lily		182 ABCDEFGHIJKLM, 228 H
Arum Lily	Folk	126 W
Arum Lily	Folk-like	182 FG
Arum Lily	Motif	182 AFG
Asparagus	Bunch	294 B
Asparagus	Motif	294 BEFG
Aubergine	Motif	289, 302 G, 308 D
Bamboo	Cane	115 G
Bamboo	Leaf	115 G
Bamboo	Motif	98 A, 111 I, 115 D
Banana		288 DEF
Banana	Peeled	288 F
Barley	Sheath	330 C, 369 CH
Bean	Motif	156 A, 292 ABCDEFGH
Bean	Pod	292 ABCDEFGH
Bean	Seed	292 ABCDFGHz
Bean	Vegetable	156 A
Bean		113 G
Beetroot	Bunch	291 G
Beetroot	Motif	291 FGHKM
Bell-like	Flower	183 ABCDGHIJKLMNPQRSTU
Berry Clusters		312
Berry-like	Structures	315, 316
Blackberry		283
Blackberry	Flower	283 D
Blackberry	Leaf	283 E
Blackberry	Stem	283 BC
Bluebell	Motif	146 B
Borders	Acanthus	39, 47 AEGKMN, 48 CFGK, 49 AIJ, 50 CDEFJK, 52 H, 56 E, 73 ACFKL, 74 BEH, 372 T, 373 AHKL, 374 MRS, 375 F
Borders	Anthemion	36 ABGKL, 38 ACD
Borders	Byzantine	55 ABCDEFGHI, 56 ABCDEFGIJK
Borders	Camellia	101 BC, 102 C
Borders	Chinese	100, 101, 102
Borders	Chrysanthemum	101 G
Borders	Cresting	73 DJKL, 74 H, 100 BCEFGJK
Borders	Daisy	16 C, 21 J, 48 M, 55 DEF, 56 JK, 69 B, 73 BIMPQT, 100 I, 101 AEFH, 102 EG, 117 AEK, 167 R, 170 A, 374 ACEFIJKLQ, 375 HIJK
Borders	Egyptian	29 ABCDFGHI
Borders	Flower	372 BDEGHIR, 373 BDIJN, 374 ABCE FIJKLOQ, 375 EGHIJKLN
Borders	Folk-like	372 E
Borders	Gothic-Tracery	57
Borders	Grape	29 FHI, 35 AG, 35 AGH, 36 CD, 47 H, 48

		DL, 49 BK, 50 B, 55 AHI, 56 F, 74 G, 155 DF, 249 R,372 J
Borders	Grape-Leaf	52 A, 56 D, 74 I, 375 O
Borders	Greek	35 ABCDEFGH, 36 ABCDEFGHIJKL, 37 ABCDEFGH, 38 ABCD
Borders	Ivy	73 DNO, 249 W, 371
Borders	Laurel	35 D
Borders	Leaf	36 E, 37 D, 48 BCFGIKH, 49 ACDFIJ, 50 CDEFHIJK, 52 AH, 55 B, 56 BDE, 73 ABCDFGHKLNO, 74 ABCEHI, 87BCD, 100 ABCHJK, 102 BDF, 117 DGM, 251 S, 372 ACFKLMOST, 373 ACEFHKLMO, 374 DGHMNRSTU, 375 ABCDFMO
Borders	Lily	47 CDI, 48 A, 49 FH, 55 G, 56 ACGI, 57, 73 R, 74 D
Borders	Lotus	21 E, 36 A, 36 FI
Borders	Lotus-Leaf	101 D
Borders	Lotus-Nile	29 AG
Borders	Lotus-Sacred	100 D
Borders	Medieval	73, 74
Borders	Mesopotamian	21 ABCDEFGHIJK
Borders	Mistletoe	159 G
Borders	Morning Glory	375 E
Borders	Oak-Leaf	247 E
Borders	Olive	35 C, 36 J
Borders	Olive-Leaf	374 G
Borders	Palmette	16 C, 21 BCDFK, 36 ABGKL, 38 ACD, 47 ABCDF, 55 C
Borders	Palm-Frond	21 I
Borders	Papyrus	29 D
Borders	Pomegranate	21 A
Borders	Romanesque	47 ABCDEFGHIJKLMN, 48 ABCDE FGHIJKLMN, 49 ABCDEFGHIJK, 50 ABCDEFGHIJK
Borders	Rose	102 H, 145 D
Borders	Tulip	152 F
Borders	Water lily	21 E, 36 A
Borders	Water lily-Nile	29 AG
Bougainvillea		218 H
Bouquet	Design	16 G, 27 F, 77 H, 137 C, 360 B, 368CD
Bouquet	Wheat	368 CD
Brinjal	See Aubergine	
Broccoli		310 G
Broccoli	Motif	310 D
Butternut	Motif	300 I, 301 I
Cabbage	Chinese	309 I
Cabbage	Cross-Section	309 B
Cabbage	Motif	309 ABCDEFGHIJ
Calla Lily	See Arum Lily	
Camellia		90 BDE, 91 BCG, 93 BCDHIKOP, 98 B,105 ABCDEFGHIJM, 106 ABCGI
Camellia	Border	101 BC, 102 C
Camellia	Motif	91 C, 94 AD, 99 B, 103, 106 ACG, 112 C
Camellia	Sprig	89
Cantaloupe	Motif	280 GHIJK
Cape Gooseberry		288 A
Capsules	Cone-like	318
Capsules	Folk	134 ABCDEFGHIJKLMNO PQ RSTUVW
Carnation		203 ABH, 204 I
Carrot	Folk-like	290 FGJ
Carrot	Motif	290 ABCDEFGHIJK
Carrots	Bunch	290 C
Cartouche	Grape-Leaf	52 E
Cauliflower	Motif	310 HIJ
Cherry	Motif	270 G
Cherry Blossom		107 ABCDEFGHIJ, 118 B
Cherry Blossom	Motif	107 ABDGHIJ, 108 ABCDEFHIJKLMN OPQRSU, 109 ABCDGIKO, 111 BCGHJ, 112 J
Chestnut	Capsule	326 M
Chilli	Motif	293 ABCDEFGI
Chrysanthemum		105 K
Chrysanthemum	Border	101 G
Chrysanthemum	Motif	94 E, 112 K
Clover	Leaf	240 KLMNPT, 256 O
Clover	Motif	161 D
Coconut	See Palm-Coconut	
Cone	Border	47 J
Cone	Motif	370 B
Cone-like-Capsule		318
Cone	Pine	327 LMQ
Conifer	Coned	18 E, 20 A
Conifer	Motif	98 C, 111 A, 115 BCH, 348 EH
Conifer	Tree	18 ACEF, 19 AFGH, 86 I, 115 BCH, 340 IJKL, 341 EGH
Corn	See Maize	
Cornucopia	Design	351, 367 BL
Cornucopia	Motif	351
Cresting	Design	67 ABIV, 73 DJKL, 74 H, 100 BCEFGJK
Cucumber	Leaf	301 L
Cucumber	Motif	301 KL
Cyclamen	Motif	144 B, 153 C, 160 C
Daffodil	Geometric	202 A
Daffodil	Motif	366 F
Dahlia	Motif	150 B
Daisy		96 E, 228 B, 128 ABCDEFGHIJKLM NOPQ, 129 ACDEFGHIJKLMOP
Daisy	Border	21 J, 29 BC, 48 M, 55 DEF, 56 JK, 69 B, 73 BIMPQT, 100 I, 101 AEFH, 102 EG, 117 AEK, 167 R, 170 A, 374 ACEFIJKLQ, 375 HIJK
Daisy	Bouquet	368 D
Daisy	Flower	14 BCDEFGHIJ, 15 B, 16 CF, 21 J, 29 BCE, 32 CDEGHJ
Daisy	Motif	32 CDEGHJ, 40 DEFGI, 43 KM, 53 IJ, 58 CFH, 59 IL, 66 A, 67 CDFGHKLMNOSW, 69 BDE FHMN, 80 CEJ, 81 FI, 94 CFGHM, 99 CEGHIJ, 106 F, 108 OT, 109 EFHJLN, 111 DEL, 112 G, 116 DH, 117 BF, 129 N, 137 CEFHJLN, 139 DEFHI, 141, 146 A, 155 I, 157 F, 160 C, 168 ABCDEFGHIJKMNOPQRS, 170 DFG, 171 BDEG, 173 D, 175 BCDE FGHJKMNOPRTVWXYZ, 176 AE, 227 FGLNOR, 352 DEHJKO, 353 ABFGH, 354 BCD, 355 DJ, 360 Y, 368 D
Daisy	Pattern	29 E, 43 J, 66 S, 69 A, 116 BEFGI, 174 ABEFGH, 355 ABEFGI, 356 BEGH
Daisy-like-flower		184 FLM, 226 BCDEGHJKLMNV

Dandelion	Leaf	241 J
Dandelion	Motif	59 M, 149 D, 153 I
Dandelion-like	Flower/Seed	224 ADFHIMNPSTUXY
Day Lily		178 E
Dog Rose	See Rose	
Fennel	Motif	302 DI
Fern	Frond	241 F
Fern	Leaf	249 P, 253 B
Festoon	Design	167 R Fig - 270 EH
Fig (Leaf)		246 GH, 270 H
Finial	Design	60 DGMNOP, 249 I, 370 B
Fir	See Conifer	
Flame Lily		228 J
Fleur de Lis	Motif	367 AFG
Flowers	Art Deco	167
Flowers	Border	372 BDEGHIR, 373 BDIJN, 374 ABCE FIJKLOQ, 375 EGHIJKLN
Flowers	Bud	223 ABCDEFGHIJKLMNOPQRSTVWXYZ
Flowers	Chinese	93
Flowers	Folk-Design	121, 122, 123, 125, 126, 127
Flowers	Folk-like	186 ABCDEFGHIJKLMNOPQRST
Flowers	Islamic	75, 76, 77, 78, 79
Flowers	Pattern	87 A
Flowers In Basket	Motif	115 A, 364 AC, 366 B
Flowers In Pot	Design	86 B, 117 B, 137 EFH, 140 F
Flowers In Urn	Design	59 N
Flowers In Vase	Design	76 J, 170 D, 176 H
Flowers In Vase	Motif	170 D, 176 H
Folk-Designs	Flower	120, 121, 122, 122, 123, 124, 125, 126, 127
Folk-Flower	Motif	127 N
Folk-like	Apple	262 CDEFKMO, 263 ABCEFI, 264 DF
Folk-like	Arum Lily	182 FG
Folk-like	Carrot	290 FGJ
Folk-like	Flower	184 ABEFGJLMNOPQST, 185 ACDE GJKMNOP, 186 ABCDEFGHIJKL MNOPQRST, 188 ABCEFGHIJKLQRTU, 202 ABCDEFGHIJKLMNOPQRSTU, 212 C, 215 ABCEIO, 218 A, 219 CEFHKOQ, 220 CEFHIKLMNO, 221 BCDFGHIJKLM PQ, 222 BDFGM
Folk-like	Flower-Bud	223 ABENOX
Folk-like	Grape	282 D
Folk-like	Lemon	286 DEF
Folk-like	Maize	295 EFH
Folk-like	Motif	358 AC
Folk-like	Onion	297 DF
Folk-like	Orange	287 L
Folk-like	Palmette	206 B
Folk-like	Pineapple	266 ABCDEFGHKLM, 267 ABCDE FGHIJKL, 268 ABCDK
Folk-like	Plum	281 BEL
Folk-like	Pomegranate	271 AC, 272 ADGJM, 273 ACEGKL, 274 BDEFGHIKM, 275 ABCDE FGHIJKLM, 276 CE, 277 EGI, 278 ACDGHJKN, 279 CDEFGHLNO
Folk-like	Rose	194 ADEFGHK, 195 ABCDEFGHIKLM NO, 196 EFHJLMO, 197 DEIJNOPQR
Folk-like	Strawberry	258 BCDHIJKL, 260 ACDEFGILM, 261ABCEFHIJ
Folk-like	Sunflower	198 ABCDEFGHIKL, 199 ABCDEGH
Folk-like	Tree-Apple	336 C
Folk-like	Tulip	191 ABLPRT, 192 ABCDEFGLNRS,193 ALMU
Folk-like	Turnip	291 IJL
Fruit	Bowl	17 G
Fruit	Motif	170 J
Fruit	Pomegranate	21 A
Fruit In Basket	Design	53 EFGK
Fruit In Basket	Motif	53 EFGK, 365 DFG
Fruit In Bowl	Design	170 C
Fruit In Bowl	Motif	137 M, 170 C, 376 N
Fruiting Bodies		323
Fruiting Capsules		311, 317, 319, 321, 325, 326, 327
Fruiting Structures		320, 324
Fruiting Structures (Cross-Section)		332
Fruiting Structures (Folk)		135 ABCDEFGHIJKLMNOPQR
Garland	Design	51, 364 BDFG
Garland	Design-Rose	166 J
Garland	Rose	166 J
Garlic	Motif	302 H
Geometric	Daffodil	202 A
Geometric	Design	77 G, 79, 80 DEFHIKLM, 81 ACGK, 86 DEFGHI, 120 CLM, 124 I, 138 ABJ, 260 C, 266 ABCDG, 267 ABCDEFGHIJKL, 295 K, 305 ABE, 306 E, 339 F, 340 ABCDEHIJLM, 344 EK, 360 V, 362 EFGI
Geometric	Design-Rose	148 E
Geometric	Flower	202 ABCDEFGHIJKLMNOPQRSTU
Geometric	Lemon	285 F
Geometric	Maize	295 K
Geometric	Motif	357 BDFGHILPQRT, 358 AC, 359 E
Geometric	Pomegranate	278 CH
Geometric	Rose	196 I, 202 OP
Geometric	Tree	339 F
Ginkgo	Leaf	158 BDFGHI, 240 R, 242 LNP
Ginkgo	Motif	158 BDFGHI, 159 H, 162 C, 240 R
Ginkgo	Sprig	159 D
Gooseberry		288 GHIJ
Gooseberry	Leaf	288 IJ
Gooseberry	Sprig	288 H
Gothic	Border	57
Gothic-Tracery	Design	66 EHIMOPQ, 68, 69 DEFHINOQR
Gourds-like		314
Grape	Border	21 GH, 29 FHI, 35 AGH, 36 CD,42 A, 47 H, 48 DL, 49 BK, 50 B, 55 AHI, 56 F, 155 DF, 249 R, 372 J
Grape	Fruit	21 GH, 27 A, 28 B, 29 FHI, 35 H, 42 AE, 43 C, 52 BF
Grape	Garland	51
Grape	Leaf	27 A, 29 HI, 33 HKL, 50 HI, 52 ABEG, 55 I, 74 GI, 82 G, 155 DF, 159 AF, 233, 241 UWX, 242 AFJ, 251 MN, 254 D, 256 HN, 282 ABCFGHKLMNO, 334 ABCDE
Grape	Motif	41 F, 66 T, 138 F, 170 B, 171 C, 282 BDEIJKMNO, 351, 365 CEFGH, 369 E
Grape	Potted	52 F
Grape	Tendril	254 D
Grape	Vine	45 DFG, 46 E, 52 F, 334 ABCDE Grape

Vine-Potted		365 H
Grape	Wreath	51
Grape-Bunch	Motif	52 B
Grape-Leaf	Border	52 A, 56 D, 375 O
Grape-Leaf	Motif	52 EG, 159 AF, 233
Grape-Vine	Motif	334 ABCDE
Grapefruit	Motif	287 JM
Grass Seeds		329
Green pepper	Motif	293 HJKLMN, 308 E
Hibiscus		218 JI
Horn Of Plenty	See Cornucopia	351
Iris		179 ABCDEFGHIJK, 228 ACD
Iris	Fleur De Lis	367 AFG
Iris	Flower	41 P
Iris	Motif	99 A, 112 A, 118 A, 144 ACD, 164 AC, 179 G
Iris	Bearded	179 CJ
Iris-Bearded	Motif	232 D
Iris-like	Flower	179 ABCDEFGHIJK, 180 ABDEFIJKLMOPQR
Ivy	Border	73 DNO, 249 W, 371
Ivy	Leaf	63 AEFIKLMO, 73 DNO, 114 K, 249 W, 251 UV
Kiwi	Fruit	288 B
Kiwi Fruit	Cross-Section	288 B
Kohlrabi		310 B
Laurel	Border	35 D
Laurel	Leaf	35 D
Leaves	Acanthus	32 BKM, 33 M, 41 ABCDEGJ, 42 CDGKL, 47 AEGKMN, 48 CFGK, 49 AIJ, 50 CDEFJK, 53 B, 56 E, 60 ADEGHIJ KLMNOPQST, 61, 66 BCFGJKLNR, 67 BIJRTU, 73 ACFKL, 74 BEH, 82 BDEIK, 244 HIMNO, 248 E, 249 AFIS, 251 L, 252 E, 253 DEFK, 254 BCEFGKL, 255 ABCDEFGHIJKLMNOPQRS
Leaves	Apple	262 NP, 263 H, 264 EFGH
Leaves	Arabesque	83, 84, 85
Leaves	Art Deco	172 G
Leaves	Bamboo	115 G
Leaves	Blackberry	283 E
Leaves	Border	36 E, 37 D, 48 BCFGIKN, 49 ACDFIJ, 50 CDEFHIJK, 52 AH, 55 B, 56 BDE, 73 ABCDFGHKLNO, 74 ABCEHI, 87 BCD, 100 ABCHJK, 102 BDF, 117 DGM, 251 S, 372 ACFKLMOST, 373 ACEFHKL MO, 374 DGHMNRSTU, 375 ABCDFMO
Leaves	Chinese	97
Leaves	Clover	161 D, 240 KLMNPT, 256 O
Leaves	Cucumber	301 L
Leaves	Dandelion	241 J
Leaves	Fern	249 P
Leaves	Fig	246 GH, 270 H
Leaves	Geometric	247 DJ
Leaves	Ginkgo	158 BDFGHI, 162 C, 240 R, 242 LNP
Leaves	Gooseberry	288 IJ
Leaves	Grape	21 H, 29 HI, 33 HKL, 48 DL, 50 HI, 52 ABEG, 55 I, 74 GI, 82 G, 155 DF, 159 AF, 233, 241 UWX, 242 AFJ, 251 MN, 254 D, 256 HN, 282 ABCFGHKLMNO, 334 ABCDE
Leaves	Islamic	82, 83, 84, 85
Leaves	Ivy	63 AEFIKLMO, 73 DNO, 114 K, 249 W, 251 UV
Leaves	Japanese	114
Leaves	Laurel	35 D
Leaves	Lemon	285 ABCDE
Leaves	Lotus-Sacred	91 ADEF, 92 D
Leaves	Maple	114 M
Leaves	Marrow	300 CJ
Leaves	Medieval	60, 60, 61, 64, 65
Leaves	Motif	66 BCDFGJKNR, 67 ABIPQRTUV, 68 D, 82 IL, 96 ABCDF, 98 FG, 99 FM, 112 EF, 114 L, 116 A, 140 KN, 149 J, 153 ABF, 157 AEF, 161 ABCDGHI, 169 BDI, 172 BCDI, 173 ADE, 176 CDEGIJ, 244 MNO, 248 N, 359 ALP, 360 FGHKLMNOTUWXZ, 361 ABCFGHN, 362 ACDL
Leaves	Mulberry	270 F
Leaves	Nasturtium	153 H
Leaves	Oak	59 B, 62 A, 64, 65, 67 AP, 69 PL, 140 H, 240 I, 243 FGHJKLMN, 244 A, 247 AE, 251 Q, 256 GIJKM, 346 ABEFI
Leaves	Olive	35 C, 36 J
Leaves	Palm	17 K, 21 I, 28 AH
Leaves	Pattern	173 B, 174 I
Leaves	Pea	244 K, 298 GJN
Leaves	Peach	257
Leaves	Pear	335 AFH
Leaves	Poppy	147 F
Leaves	Raspberry	283 E
Leaves	Romanesque	44
Leaves	Rose	142 CDG
Leaves	Strawberry	259 DFN
Leaves	Stylised	234, 235, 236, 237, 238, 239, 240, 241, 242, 243, 244, 245, 246, 247, 248, 249, 250, 252, 253, 254, 255, 256
Leaves	Thistle	252 C
Leaves	Tomato	303 A, 306 B, 307 JM
Leek	Motif	297 H
Legumes	Fruiting Body	322
Lemon	Cross-Section	284 ABGH, 285 ACDEFGI, 286 ACDEFGHI
Lemon	Folk-like	286 DEF
Lemon	Geometric	285 F
Lemon	Leaf	285 ABCDE
Lemon	Motif	284 ABCEFGH, 285 ABCDEFGHI, 286 ABCDEFGHI
Lemon	Quartered	284 F
Lemon	Seed	286 GI
Lemon	Sprig	284 C
Lemon	Tree	284 D
Lettuce	Motif	310 ACEF
Lily		63 CHJ, 145 E, 178, 181 ABCDE FGHIJKLM
Lily	Border	47 CDI, 48 A, 49 FH, 55 G, 56 ACGI, 57, 73 R, 74 D
Lily	Bud	62 CDGHIJLQX
Lily	Flower	22 D, 25 H, 58 ABDEGIKLM, 59CDEFHKLN
Lily	Garland	51
Lily	Motif	22 D, 25 H, 52 DI, 56 H, 59 LN, 77 H, 80

		AF, 146 BCE, 178 L, 181 K
Lily	Pattern	69 C
Lily	Potted	59 N
Lily	Wreath	51
Lily-Arum		182 ABCDEFGHIJKLM
Lily-Arum	Motif	182 AFG
Lily-like-flower		178 ABCDEFGHIJKL, 181 ABCDEFGHIJK LM, 185ACEGHIJKMNPQ
Lily	Madonna	181 I
Lily Of The Valley	Motif	151 E, 162 D
Lotus	Border	21 E, 36 A, 36 FI, 37 AC, 38 BCD Lotus
Bud		21 E, 23, 24 EH
Lotus	Flower	15 I, 16 GH, 23, 24 AEHJ, 27 ABCDEF
Lotus	Motif	34 B
Lotus-Leaf	Border	101 D
Lotus-Nile	Bud	27 BDF
Lotus-Nile	Flower	25 GJ, 28 CEGJ, 29 AG
Lotus-Nile	Motif	28 GJ
Lotus-Sacred		91 ADEF
Lotus-Sacred	Border	100 D
Lotus-Sacred	Bud	92 D
Lotus-Sacred	Motif	91 ADEF, 92 D
Lotus-Sacred (Seed Capsule)		92 D
Madonna Lily		181 I
Maidenhair Tree	See Ginkgo	
Maize	Folk-like	295 EFH
Maize	Geometric	295 K
Maize	Motif	295 ABCDEFGHIJKL, 296 ABCDEFGHI, 369 G
Maize	Plant	295 J
Maize	Sheath	369 G
Mandorla	Design	67 P
Maple	Leaf	114 M
Marrow	Cross-Section	300 B
Marrow	Flower	300 CH, 302 ABCEF
Marrow	Leaf	300 CJ
Marrow	Motif	300 ABCDEFGHIJ
Medallion	Design	14 ADEHJ, 32 CL, 40 GHI, 53 H, 67 CDFHKLMNOSW, 68 ABCDEFHIJKLMNOPQ, 111 ABCE FGHKL, 112 AEGH, 147 A, 354 EFJPQR
Melon		95 F
Mistletoe		59 E
Mistletoe	Border	159 G
Mistletoe	Motif	158 C, 159 B
Morning Glory	Border	375 E
Morning Glory	Motif	213 E
Morning Glory	Sprig	145 H
Mulberry		270 F
Mulberry	Leaf	270 F
Mushroom	Motif	113 DE, 294 ACDHIJLKLMNOP
Nasturtium		160 G
Nasturtium	Leaf	153 H
Nasturtium	Motif	153 GH
Oak	Acorns	327 BCDEGHIJ
Oak	Bough	247 A
Oak	Leaf	62 A, 64, 65, 66 D, 67 AP, 140 H, 240 I, 243 FGHJKLMN, 244 A, 247 AE, 251 Q, 256 GIJKM, 346 ABEFI

Oak	Tree	71 CDEHI, 72 AJ, 346 AEFI
Oak Leaf	Motif	367 H
Oak Acorn	Motif	59 B
Oak Leaf	Border	247 E
Oak Leaf	Motif	59 B, 67 AP, 69 L, 240 I
Oak Leaf	Pattern	69 P
Oak Tree	Motif	71 CDEHI, 72 AJ
Oats	Sheath	369 AF
Octagonal	Design	32 G
Olive	Border	35 C, 36 J
Olive	Leaf	35 C
Olive	Sprig	34 H
Olive-Leaf	Border	374 G
Onion	Cross-Section	297 BDF
Onion	Folk-like	297 DF
Onion	Motif	297 ABCDEFGIJK
Orange	Cross-Section	287 ACDEHL
Orange	Folk-like	287 L
Orange	Motif	287 ABCDEFGHIKL
Orange	Sprig	287 K
Orange	Tree	337 BD
Oranges	Pattern	176 B
Orange-Tree	Motif	337 BD
Paisley	Pattern	206 ABCDEFGHIJKL
Palm	Frond	14 A, 21 I
Palm	Leaf	17 K, 21 I
Palm	Motif	140 CE, 344 I
Palm	Tree	70 ABDGH, 339 A, 350 E
Palm-Coconut	Motif	344 AH
Palm-Coconut	Tree	344 AH
Palm-Date		28 AH
Palm-Date	Fruiting	20 ACG, 20 DE, 30 AB, 54 ACE, 342 ADFH, 343 ABDGI
Palm-Date	Geometric	344 EK
Palm-Date	Leaf	28 AH
Palm-Date	Motif	53 L, 54 ACDE, 342 ABCDEFGH, 343 ABCDEFGHI, 344 BCDEFGJK
Palm-Date	Tree	15 AC, 16 ADE, 20 ABCABCDEFGHI, 30 ABD, 53 DL, 54 ACDE, 86 C, 343 ABCDEFGHI, 344 BCDEFGJK
Palm-Fan	Tree	339 B
Palmette	Border	21 BCDFK, 36 ABGKL, 37 ABCEG, 47 ABCDF, 55 C
Palmette	Design	13, 15 EFGHJK, 20 BDFH, 22 C, 31, 32 FI, 33 ABCDEFGIJ, 34 ACDE, 35 BE, 36 ABGKL, 37 ABCEG, 38 ACD, 47 ABCDF, 66 BC, 76 CFGK, 79 B, 82 L, 206 ABCDEFGHIJKL
Palmette	Folk-like	206 B
Palmette	Motif	66 BC
Pansy	Motif	149 H
Papaw	Cross-Section	288 C, 288 C
Papaw	Tree	339 C
Papyrus	Bud	28 F, 29 D
Papyrus	Grass	24 BCDFGIK, 25 KLM, 26 ABCDE FGHIJKLMN, 27 ABCG, 28 FI, 29 D
Papyrus	Motif	25 LM, 27 B
Pea		298 ABCDEFGHIJKLMN

Pea	Flower	298 HJM
Pea	Leaf	244 K, 298 GJN
Pea	Motif	136 B, 298 ABCDEFIJKL, 299 ABCDE FGHIJKLMNO
Pea	Pod	136 B, 298 ABCDEFILKL, 299 ABCDE FGHIJKLMNO
Pea	Seed	298 ADEIL, 299 BCEGIKMN
Peace Lily		28 N
Peach	Motif	95 DEJ, 111 K, 113 C, 257
Peach	Sprig	95 DEJ
Peach	Tree	345 C
Peach Blossom	Motif	99 L
Peach Blossom	Sprig	92 AEF
Pear	Cross-Section	265 BFHIJKL
Pear	Leaf	335 AFH
Pear	Motif	136 A, 265 ABCDEFGHIJKL, 365 AE
Pear	One Third	265 G
Pear	Quartered	265 E
Pear	Seed	265 EGIJKL
Pear	Tree	54 B, 72 C
Pear Tree	Motif	54 B, 265 C, 335 AFH
Peony	Motif	90 AC
Persimmon	Motif	113 F
Pine	Cone	16 H
Pine Cone		327 LMQ
Pineapple	Cross-Section	266 DFHIJK, 267 GIK, 269 CDF, 270 C
Pineapple	Folk-like	266 ABCDEFGHKLM, 267 ABCDE FGHIJKL, 268 ABCDK
Pineapple	Geometric	266 ABCDG, 267 ABCDEFGHIJKL
Pineapple	Motif	136 DF, 170 J, 266 ABCDEFGHIJKLM, 267 ABCDEFGHIJKL, 268 ABCDE FGHIJKL, 269 ABCDEF, 270 ABCDE
Pineapple	Peeled	270 E
Pip	Plum	281 ACFGJ
Plaque	Design	99 ABJL, 117 BCFJ
Plum	Folk-like	281 BEL
Plum	Motif	281 ABCDEFGHIJKL
Plum	Pip	281 ACFGJ
Pod	Bean	292 ABCDEFGH
Pod	Fruiting Body	322
Pod	Pea	298 ABCDEFILKL
Pod	Pea-Vegetable	299 ABCDEFGHIJKLMNO
Pomegranate		113 AHI, 271 ABCDEF, 272 ABCDE FGHIJKLMNOPQR, 273 ABCDEFGHIJKL, 274 ABCDEFGHIJKLMN, 275 ABCDE FGHIJKLM, 276 ABCDE, 277 ABCDEFGHIJ, 278 ABCDEFGHIJKLMN, 279 ABCDE FGHIJKLMN, 136 GHIJKL
Pomegranate	Border	21 A
Pomegranate	Capsule	317 AEGLQRUW
Pomegranate	Folk-like	271 AC, 272 ADGJM, 273 ACEGKL, 274 BDEFGHIKM, 276 CE, 277 EGI, 278 ACDGHJKN, 279 CDEFGHLNO
Pomegranate	Fruit	17 FH, 21 A, 41 O, 79 D
Pomegranate	Geometric	79 D, 278 CH
Pomegranate	Motif	95 HK, 113 H, 151 F, 271 BDF, 272 OR, 273 ABCDEFHJKL, 275 M, 277 D, 278 LM, 335 B, 365 BCF, 370 D
Pomegranate	Sprig	95 HK, 279 M
Pomegranate	Tree	335 A
Poppy		209 K
Poppy	Bouquet	368 C
Poppy	Bud	147 FH
Poppy	Capsule	326 CKPQS
Poppy	Leaf	147 F
Poppy	Motif	147 ABCDEFGH, 368 CEG
Poppy	Seed Capsule	147 AH
Posy	Design	359 Q
Potato		308 CFGH
Potato	Flower	308 G
Pumpkin	Cross-Section	301 BCGI
Pumpkin	Flower	302 ABCEF
Pumpkin	Motif	301 ABCDEFGJM, 363 G
Radish	Motif	291 ABCD
Raspberry		283
Raspberry	Flower	283 D
Raspberry	Leaf	283 E
Raspberry	Stem	283 BC
Raspberry/Blackberry	Motif	156 C
Rectangle	Design	16 AB, 40 M, 43 GHL, 56 H, 99 ABJLM, 142 E, 151 D, 155 BJ, 171 ACE, 362 ACI JLM, 365 H
Rectangle	Design-Tulip	152 E
Reed	Stem	241 GSY, 249 NO, 251 CD
Reed Mace	See Rush	
Rhododendron		106 H
Rose		79 ACFGJKLN, 166 ABCDEFGHIJKLM NO, 175 AILQ, 176 HK, 194 ABCDE FGHIJKLMNO, 196 ABCDEFGHIJKLM NO, 197 DEGHIJMNOPQ, 201 AKL, 132 ABCDEFGHIJKL, 133 ABCDE FGHIJKLMNOPQ
Rose	Border	102 H, 145 D
Rose	Bud	124 CDEFGHIJKLMNOPQ, 133 CDHIJO, 166 ADO, 195 AABCDE FGHIJKLMNOPQRST
Rose	Bush	336 B
Rose	Folk-like	194 ADEFGHK, 195 ABCDEFGHIKLMNO, 196 EFHJLMO, 197 DEIJNOPQR, 204 C
Rose	Garland	166 J, 364 G
Rose	Geometric	135 E, 202 OP
Rose	Hip (Berry)	133 P, 197 ABCFKLR
Rose	Leaf	142 CDG
Rose	Motif	40 F, 79 ACFGJKLN, 80 BDHIKM, 81 G, 94 BIJ, 98 E, 133 ABEGN, 138 M, 142 ABCDEGIJK, 148 ABCDFGH, 163 H, 166 EFHJK, 171 H, 194 ABCDE FGHIJKLMNO, 196 CDEJLO, 197 EJQ, 201 AK, 221 P, 229 I, 355 AGL, 357 FJ, 362 NO, 363 D, 367 D, 368 B
Rose	Pattern	174 D
Rose	Silhouette	195 MO
Rose	Stem	142 FH
Rose	Swag	368 B
Rose	Thorn	142 FH
Rose-Bud	Geometric	124 I

Term	Subterm	References
Rose-Bud	Motif	124 I, 195 CFGKLPT
Rose-Bush	Motif	336 B
Rose-Dog		196 DIK, 197 I
Rose-Dog	Motif	142 ABCG, 148 ABCG, 194 CEGKLNO, 354 P
Rose Hip	Capsule	197 ABCFKLR, 317 DF
Rosette	Acanthus	53 B
Rosette	Design	14 BCEFGHIJ, 32 CBDEGHJKL, 40 DEFGI, 52 DG, 53 BIJ, 58 CFH, 66 E, 67 CDFGHKLMNO, 68, 79 FGI, 80 BDEFHKM, 94 ABCDEFGHIJKLM, 108 BCGJOPQRSTU, 109 ABDEHIJKLO, 111 D, 112 CDHK, 137 JN, 138 EM, 139 ADEFHIJMN, 142 B, 153 E, 168 ABCDEGIJKMNOS, 177, 194 ABCDE FGHIJKLMNO, 201 A, 211 EFG, 226 CDEFIMNP, 352 ABCDFGHIJKLMNOPQ, 353 ABCDEFGHIJKL, 354 ABCE FGHIKLMNOP, 355 ABCEFGHIKL, 356 ABCDEFGHIJ, 359 CDMRS, 360 C
Rosette	Morning Glory & Daisy 177	
Rosette	Motif	58 CFH, 81 FGIKN, 227 ABCDEFGHIN PQRS, 229 BIF
Rush		329 I
Scabiosa		224 LRQW
Seed	Bean	292 ABCDFGH
Seed	Lemon	286 GI
Seed	Pea	299 BCEGIKMN
Seed	Pea-Vegetable	298 ADEIL
Seed	Tomato	303 BCD, 304 ABCDF, 305 ABCDEF, 306 ACDEF
Seed	Apple	262 AEGIJ
Seed	Pear	265 EGIJKL
Seed	Sycamore	160 C
Seed Capsules		313
Sheath	Design	330 ACJM, 368 EG, 369 ABCDEFGH, 369 CH
Sheath	Wheat	368 EG, 369 BED
Silhouette	Design	66 EHIMOP, 68 ABCEFGHIJKLMNOPQ, 195 MO, 207 D, 208 BDNS, 360 ACIM RUVWZ
Sprig	Apple	262 BFN, 263 H
Sprig	Design-Ginkgo	159 D
Sprig	Gooseberry	288 H
Sprig	Lemon	284 C
Sprig	Orange	287 K
Sprig	Pomegranate	279 M
Sprig	Tomato	306 B, 307 J
Sprig, Apple	Design	95 B, 113 B
Sprig, Camellia	Design	89, 91 BG
Sprig, Cherry Blossom (Design)		107 BCDGHIJ, 111 J, 118 B
Sprig, Conifer	Design	115 F
Sprig, Ivy	Design	63 LMO
Sprig, Oak	Design	59 B
Sprig, Peach Blossom (Design)		92 AEF
Sprig, Peony	Design	90 C
Sprig, Pomegranate (Design)		95 HK, 113 AI
Sprig, Viburnum	Design	92 C
Square	Design	16 FGH, 32 B, 43 K, 53 AC, 86 G, 117 BCFJ, 142 ACK, 155 AH, 171 BF, 263 P, 273 DHJ, 287 I, 359 EF, 360 ST, 362 BDEHKNO, 365 ABC
Square	Design, Rose	148 E
Square	Design, Tulip	152 ABG
Squash	Motif	301 H
Stellar	Design	14 CDEI, 66 HM, 81 GJK, 370 A
Stem		173 C, 251 ABCDGIK, 249 CENO
Stem	Acanthus	255 CIJKMNR
Stem	Blackberry	283 BC
Stem	Raspberry	283 BC
Stem	Rose	142 FH
Stem	Reed	241 GSY
Strawberry		259, 261
Strawberry	Flower	259 HJMO
Strawberry	Folk-like	258 BCDHIJKL, 260 ACDEFGILM, 261 ABCEFHIJ
Strawberry	Geometric	260 C
Strawberry	Leaf	259 DFN
Strawberry	Motif	258 ABCDEFGHIJKL, 259 CFINP, 260 ABCDEFGHIJKLM, 261 ACEGIKL, 365 D
Strawberry	Plant	259 N
Sunflower		90 F, 198 ABCDEFGHIJKL, 199 ABCDE FGHIJ
Sunflower	Folk-like	198 ABCDEFGHIKL, 199 ABCDEGH
Sunflower	Motif	198 GIL, 199 EFGIJ, 358 F, 367 E
Swag	Design	367 CM, 368 B
Sycamore	Seed	160 C
Tangerine	Motif	287 N
Teasel		62 R
Thistle	Leaf	252 C
Thistle	Motif	358 D
Thistle-like flower		189 ABCDEFGHIJKLMNOPQR, 190 ABCDEFGHIJKLMNOPQRS
Thistle-like fruiting structures		328
Thistle	Spear	190 OQ
Thorn	Rose	142 FH
Tomato	Cross-Section	303 BCD, 304 ABCEF, 305 ABCDEF, 306 ACDEF, 306 ACDEF, 307 ACDEFK
Tomato	Flower	307 GJ
Tomato	Geometric	305 ABE, 306 E
Tomato	Leaf	303 A, 306 B, 307 JM
Tomato	Motif	156 EF, 303 ABCD, 304 ABCDEF, 305 ABCDEF, 306 ABCDEF, 307 ABCDEFHIJKLM
Tomato	Plant	303 A
Tomato	Seed	303 BCD, 304 ABCDF, 305 ABCDEF, 306 ACDEF
Tomato	Sprig	306 B, 307 J
Topiary	Motif	ADEF, 338 AB
Tracery	Design	112 I
Tree of Life	Design	88
Tree-fruiting	Motif	334 F
Trees	Apple	71 AG, 335 CDEG, 347 B, 348 AD
Trees	Art Deco	172 AEFH
Trees	Byzantine	54 ABCDE
Trees	Camellia	89
Trees	Coned	18 E
Trees	Conifer	18 ACEF, 19 AFGH, 86 I, 98 C, 111 A, 115 BCH, 340 IJKL, 341 EGH, 348 EH
Trees	Egyptian	30 ABCD
Trees	Flowering	19 I, 45 AC, 70 I, 86 F, 88, 140 AB, 160 A, 336, 337 C, 338 A, 340 BFGH, 341 BCF,

		345 BE, 346 DHKL
Trees	Fruiting	140 GM, 333, 340 JKLM, 345 F
Trees	Geometric	18 A, 86 EFGHI, 339 F, 340 ABCDEHI JLM, 344 EK, 358 A
Trees	Islamic	86
Trees	Lemon	284 D
Trees	Medieval	70, 71, 72
Trees	Mesopotamian	18 ABCDEFGH, 19 ABCDEFGHI, 20 ABCDEFGHI
Trees	Motif	13, 43 D, 70, 71, 72, 86 ACEFGHI, 88, 140 ABCEGLM, 157 D, 160 A, 161 F, 172 EF, 176 F, 284 D, 333, 335 ABCDEFGH, 336 ABCDEF, 337 ABCDEF, 338 ABCDE, 340 ABCDEFGHIJKLM, 341 ABCDEFGH, 342 ABCDEFGH, 343 ABCDEFGHI, 344 ABCDEFGHIJKLMNO, 345 ABCDEF, 346 ACDEFGHIJKL, 347 ABCDEFGHIJK, 348, 349 ABCDEF, 350 ABCDEF, 358 A, 389 ABCDEF
Trees	Oak	71 CDEHI, 72 AJ, 345 AD, 346 AEFI
Trees	Orange	337 BD
Trees	Palm	53 DL, 70 ABDGH, 339 A, 344 I
Trees	Palm-Coconut	344 AH
Trees	Palm-Date	13, 15 AC, 16 ADE, 20 ABCDEFGHI, 54 ACDE, 86 C, 342 ABCDEFGH, 343 ABCDEFGHI, 344 BCDEFGJK
Trees	Palm-Fan	339 B
Trees	Papaw	339 C
Trees	Peach	345 C
Trees	Pear	54 B, 72 C, 265 C
Trees	Pomegranate	335 B
Trees	Potted	16 DE, 336 ABCDEF, 337 ABCDEF, 338 ABCDE
Trees	Romanesque	45, 46 ABCDEFGHIJ
Trees	Topiary	337 ABDEF
Trees	Tree of Life	88
Trees	Willow-Weeping	86 AG, 115 I, 140 L
Trees-flowering	Motif	338 A
Triangular	Design	66 NQ, 171 G, 262 L, 285 B, 361 CN
Tulip		120 ABCDEFGHIJKLMN, 191 DGIJKQRST, 229 A
Tulip	Border	152 F
Tulip	Bud	191 ACINQ
Tulip	Folk-like	191 ABLPRT, 192 ABCDEFGLNRS, 193 ALMU
Tulip	Geometric	120 CLM
Tulip	Motif	117 B, 119, 120 BCIJLMN, 138 BD, 142 G, 143 ABCDEFG, 152 ABCDEFG, 155 B, 163 F, 201 JN, 336 E, 354 JS, 358 EC, 363 E, 366 CG
Tulip-like flower		191 ABCDEFGHIJKLMNOPQRST, 192 ABCDEFGHIJKLMNOPQRSTU, 193 ABCDEFGHIJKLMNOPQRSTUV
Turnip		291 JILE
Turnip	Bunch	291 J
Turnip	Folk-like	291 IJL
Venus Fly Trap		218 G
Viburnum		92 C, 118 D
Water lily		204 E
Water lily	Border	21 E, 36 A, 37 AC, 38 BCD
Water lily	Bud	21 E, 24 EH
Water lily	Flower	15 I, 16 GH, 23, 24 AEHJ
Water lily	Motif	34 B, 53 C, 150 D, 153 D, 156 B, 162 A, 232 ABC
Water lily-Nile	Bud	27 BDF
Water lily-Nile	Flower	25 GJ, 27 ABCDEF, 28 CEGJ, 29 AG
Water lily-Nile	Motif	28 GJ
Watermelon	Motif	280 ABCDEF
Wheat		157 C, 330 ABDEFGHILKLMN
Wheat	Ear	17 ABCDEJLM, 25 E, 330 BDEGH, 331 ABDEHIM
Wheat	Garland	51
Wheat	Motif	147 G, 368 ACDEG
Wheat	Seed	331 CJKLNO
Wheat	Sheath	330 AJM, 368 EG
Wheat	Wreath	51
Willow-Weeping	Motif	86 AG, 140 L
Willow-Weeping	Tree	115 I
Wisteria		115 E
Wreath	Design	51, 53 I, 364 E
Yarrow		149 E
Yarrow	Flower	163 C
Yarrow	Motif	145 G
Zinnia		222 K